all you knead is
bread

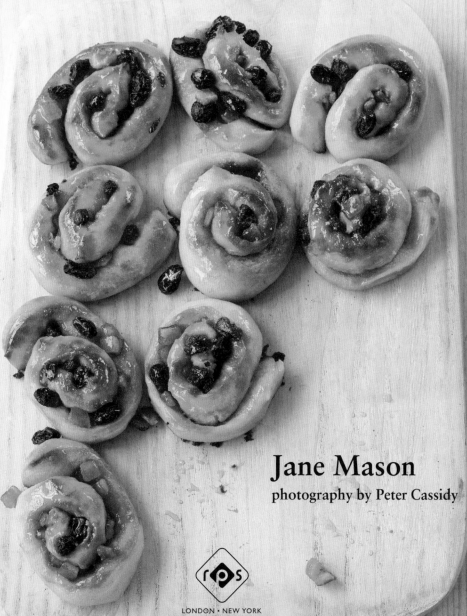

all you knead is

bread

*over 50 recipes from around the world
to bake & share*

Jane Mason

photography by Peter Cassidy

rps

LONDON • NEW YORK

This book is for my parents, who taught me
how to love cooking, baking and eating.

Picture Editor Iona Hoyle
Picture Researcher Christina Borsi
Production Manager Gordana Simakovic
Art Director Leslie Harrington
Editorial Director Julia Charles

Prop Stylists Róisín Nield and
Tony Hutchinson

US Recipe Tester Susan Stuck
Indexer Hilary Bird

First published in 2012 by
Ryland Peters & Small
20–21 Jockey's Fields
London WC1R 4BW
and
519 Broadway, 5th Floor
New York, NY 10012

www.rylandpeters.com

10 9 8 7 6 5 4 3 2 1

Text © Jane Mason 2012.
Design © Ryland Peters & Small 2012.
Commissioned photography by Peter
Cassidy © Ryland Peters & Small 2012.
See page 176 for further picture credits.

Printed in China

ISBN: 978-1-84975-257-2

A CIP record for this book is available
from the British Library.

A CIP record for this book is available
from the US Library of Congress.

Notes

• All spoon measurements are level unless
otherwise specified.

• All eggs are medium (UK) or large (US)
unless otherwise specified.

• Ovens should be preheated to the
specified temperatures. All ovens work
slightly differently. We recommend using
an oven thermometer and suggest you
consult the maker's handbook for any
special instructions, particularly if you are
cooking in a fan-assisted/convection oven,
as you will need to adjust temperatures
according to manufacturer's instructions.

Contents

Bread is a common currency

About a zillion years ago, early humans crushed up grains, kernels and seeds, mixed them with water, and cooked them to make something to eat. What they crushed determined what they ate both at the beginning of time and several thousand years later when we first started to bake.

The story of bread in our lives is at the heart of three other stories: grain, travel and settlement. Grain because most bread is made out of grain; travel because nomads, early explorers, conquering armies and settlers carried what they needed when they moved around, and integrated what they found into their lives if it enriched them; and settlement because peace and prosperity enabled bakers to develop their craft, making bread delicious and beautiful as well as functional.

Today, wheat is one of the largest cultivated grain crops, and the main ingredient in the vast majority of bread that is eaten around the world. This indicates simply that it grows like a weed. From its birthplace as a cultivated grain somewhere between what were then Mesopotamia and Eastern Anatolia/the Western Armenian Highlands around 6,000 BCE, wheat has conquered almost the entire world, moving around the fertile crescent, across to Asia, up to Europe, and over oceans to the Americas, Australia, Africa and New Zealand. There are few places where wheat and bread made from wheat flour have not thrived.

There are plenty of other grains in the world including amaranth, barley, buckwheat, corn, flax, millet, oats, quinoa, rice, rye and teff. They are all delicious and nutritious and are used to make all sorts of food including bread. However, some require special growing conditions (water, cold, heat or altitude), others originated in countries that neither spawned nor experienced the kinds of explorers who popularized these grains in the way wheat has been popularized, and none can be stretched to create the variety of shapes or the fluffy light texture that are associated with stability. Only wheat can do that.

The mass movement of people in the last hundred years no longer spread grains and seeds, but it has spread bread. Most immigrants miss bread more than anything else in their countries of origin and, once established in new homes, many set up bakeries and introduced their bread and bread customs to their new home countries. This is why you can get tortillas in China, steamed buns in Paris, baguettes in Delhi, naan bread in Rome, ciabatta in Hamburg, rye bread in Montreal…

Sadly, highly processed bread, rapidly baked by 'plant bakers' has also marched around the world. Square, spongy and soft, this product smells a bit like vinegar, forms a gooey ball if you squeeze it, sticks to the roof of your mouth when you eat it, and simply does not taste like bread. It is time that we demanded something better, or started baking bread ourselves.

Bread is a basic staple, an occasional treat, an inexpensive luxury and a key part of celebration and ritual. It is a metaphor for money and, in many languages, the words for bread and life, joy and celebration are interchangeable. Bread is the stuff of story, song and poetry, and is a symbol for everything that is basic and necessary. To waste bread is a sin. To make and share it is a blessing. On their own, the basic ingredients – flour, water, salt and yeast – do not sustain us. They are only life-giving when combined. Good bread is the result of responsible farming, gentle milling, an element of hand baking and local delivery with minimal packaging. It is a window into culture, affirming both our individuality and humanity.

Observing this makes it clear that the decisions we take about the kinds of bread we make, buy and eat can change the world for better or worse.

Understanding bread ingredients

Basic bread is made of flour and water. Yeast makes it rise and salt makes it taste better. Out of these ingredients you can make endless varieties of bread. You can expand your repertoire exponentially if you choose to add and/or substitute ingredients. You don't have to be an expert before you substitute wine for water or add raisins. However, there are a few things you may want to know before you begin. They are outlined in the following pages and will be an invaluable guide on you new bread-baking journey.

Flour

You can bake a kind of bread out of almost any flour, although different kinds of flour behave in different ways.

Gluten in flour is like a balloon, expanding as the carbon dioxide is expelled by the yeast. Flour with gluten includes wheat (and its cousins spelt, emmer, kamut and einkorn), rye and barley. Flour that may contain gluten includes oat and hemp (read the label carefully if this is important to you). All other kinds of flour are gluten free.

It is important to know a bit about gluten. Firstly, different types of flour are not necessarily interchangeable and secondly, some people are mildly or severely gluten intolerant. This intolerance, called coeliac disease, affects a small minority of the population and the symptoms can be mild (tummy ache) to severe (neuropathy). This book has some gluten-free recipes for things like fritters, pancakes and 'skillet bread' but does not have recipes for gluten-free bread baked as a loaf. There are some great recipes for this kind of bread in Emmanuel Hadjiandreou's excellent book *How to Make Bread*.

Different kinds of flour behave in different ways

The vast majority of bread that is eaten around the world is made from white wheat flour which, in most of the English-speaking world, is categorized by its strength, ie. the amount of gluten it contains.

Very strong bread flour has a high gluten content, is very stretchy, rises well, and makes great, sturdy bread.

Plain or all-purpose flour is a bit weaker, less stretchy and will not rise as much as very strong flour – it makes bread with a softer texture.

Cake and pastry flour is weaker again, even less stretchy, and does not make great bread although it does make great cake and pastry (funny that).

Rye flour does not have stretchy gluten and

cannot really be shaped at all. Gluten-free flours need to be handled much like cake mixture. Even spelt, emmer, kamut and einkorn – wheat's older cousins – will behave differently from wheat. You can substitute them for wheat in any recipe but be prepared to adjust.

Wholemeal/whole-wheat flour (flour made from the whole grain) performs a little differently from white flour. The bran and germ run interference in the dough, making it less stretchy and heavier.

Different types of flour make different kinds of dough and different styles of bread. Even if you stick to one kind of flour, you have to remember that from season to season and field to field, grain differs, and from bag to bag, flour differs. Every time you change the brand or the bag of flour that you use, you will notice a difference.

Further, countries categorize flour in different ways. This is one of the reasons it is difficult to replicate bread from place to place. Shopping for flour can be confusing, and good-quality flour is not always easy to find. Healthfood stores are often the best places to get flour and the owner can usually advise you.

Thankfully, flour is relatively cheap, so disasters are not expensive. Besides, everything is good toasted. Even if it's ugly.

Stone milling

Stone mills process grain more gently than most industrial mills. The result is a better product from both a performance and a nutritional perspective.

Further, because mill stones (see photo, below) are 'dressed' by the miller by hand, every mill stone and, thus, all stone-milled flour is unique to the miller. There is individuality and humanity in stone-milled flour and although it is dearer, I am certain you will decide it is worth it.

If you would like to know more about flour, the Real Bread Campaign in the UK is an excellent resource.

Yeast

Yeast is a micro-organism that lives in the air. It is all around us and its job is to ferment things, breaking them down. We learned to cultivate yeast so that we could actually hold it in our hands in the mid 1800s. Before that, all bread was baked using natural yeast trapped in a paste of flour and water, ie. sourdough. These days, we have four kinds of yeast to choose from: instant, dry, fresh or sourdough.

The same quantity of flour requires different amounts of instant, dry or fresh yeast to make it rise. Quantities for each kind are given with each recipe. Do use the amount that is called for – you simply don't need more. Please don't get freaked out by yeast. The only thing that kills yeast is heat, so don't mix it with anything hot. Instructions that tell you to use warm water, or put your dough in the airing cupboard or resist slamming the door when dough is rising are simply misguided. Yeast is not that sensitive or vulnerable.

Instant or easy-bake yeast

This looks like a fine powder. The benefits include: long shelf life, easy availability, and no proofing required. You measure it into the bowl and get going straightaway, saving yourself 10–15 minutes. However, instant yeast is about 93% yeast and 7% additives of various kinds. You may want to explore what those additives are and what they do in order to make an informed choice about using instant yeast.

Dry or active dry yeast

This looks like little pellets. The benefits of dry yeast include: no additives and long shelf life. However, it is getting harder to find and it normally requires 'proofing' which adds an extra 10–15 minutes to the preparation time.

Fresh yeast

This looks like a beige eraser. The benefits of fresh yeast include: no additives and no 'proofing' required. However, it can be difficult to find and it has a short shelf life. You must keep it in the fridge and it is only good for about three weeks, but you can freeze it if you are in danger of not using it before its shelf life is up.

Natural yeast

We cannot see natural yeast because it is trapped in its paste of flour and water that is a live sourdough culture. See pages 20–27 for more information, a couple of recipes including how to make sourdough starters, and some guidance on how to adapt 'normal' bread recipes into sourdough recipes.

Water

Just about the only thing that kills yeast is heat. Using cold water to prepare dough is 100% safe.

Because all flours are different, water quantities are only ever a guide. The quantities given in these recipes are for the flour I use and I need to adjust them from time to time. I have given the metric measurements for water in grams rather than millilitres simply because it tends to be more accurate but please do not

worry too much about it. Start with the quantities given, then knead or stir. If you need to, adjust the ingredients to get a soft dough that is a pleasure to knead. If your dough is a little sticky, it does not mean you need more flour. Persevere, take a deep breath and keep going – you have not done anything wrong.

Salt

Whether you add sea salt or table salt is up to you, however, do add salt because bread with salt is not just boring, it's dreadful.

Optional extras
Milk

Enriched bread calls for milk that has been warmed. The milk is not warmed in order to proof the yeast. It is warmed because the sugars in milk break down and the flavour changes when you warm it. When this is called for, heat the milk to just below boiling point and let it cool completely before using it.

Spices

Spices are lovely in bread but go easy on them – you want bread eaters to say, 'yummy what did you put in this!', not 'wow, this tastes like curry!' Follow the recipes at first and then, if you like stronger flavoured bread, do add more.

Butter

When you add butter to bread dough, you want the flour to absorb all the butter before it melts. If a lot of butter is called for, you should knead all the ingredients for 10 minutes except the butter. Then add the butter and knead for 10 minutes more. The recipes will guide you.

Seeds, grains, dried fruit and nuts

Seeds and grains can break teeth, suck moisture out of your dough and be difficult to digest, so soak and drain them before you add them. Dried fruit also sucks a lot of moisture out of the dough and is more succulent if you soak it first. Dry-roast nuts then allow to cool before using to bring out their flavour.

Understanding bread activities

There are as many ways to make bread as there are to fall off the proverbial log. I developed my style over years of wandering around the world baking with different bakers, and it works for me. I hope it works for you too but if you have an approach that gets you results with which you are happy, don't change them. In any case, please go to www.virtuousbread.com and check out the videos for help on some of the basic activities involved in making bread.

Mixing

Bread recipes will begin by asking you to measure out some or all the ingredients, and to mix them together in a big bowl. Some recipes call for a 'predough' that you make anywhere from one hour to one day in advance. To that end, do read through the recipes thoroughly before you start.

Adding yeast

The recipes will give you clear instructions regarding how to use different kinds of yeast. Please follow them to get the best results.

Kneading

Once you have mixed all the ingredients in the bowl according to the recipe, scrape the dough directly onto a clean surface and knead it for a good 10 minutes or as stated in the recipe. Gluten is like a balloon and the first thing you do to a balloon before you blow it up is stretch it so you can blow it up more easily. Kneading is the same. It is simply stretching, and you can stretch the dough any way you like: one-handed, two-handed, in the air, with your knuckles, using a dough scraper, folding over and over – just be sure you give the dough a good stretch for at least 10 minutes.

I like to knead and I like the results it gets. There are 'no-knead' methods and they have plenty of merits but in this book most recipes ask you to knead. You can knead by hand or by machine. Generally, a dough hook is a better option than a paddle unless you are kneading dough with a high rye content, in which case use a paddle and stop part-way through to turn the dough over by hand in the mixing bowl.

It's worthwhile to knead by hand the first time you do a recipe so you can feel for the texture the recipe seeks. Set a timer because it's easy to cheat! Listen to the radio, talk to someone, dream a little and relax.

While you knead, the ingredients come together and the dough begins to transform. You will observe that it changes from a sticky, ragged mess to a slightly sticky, silky, stretchy parcel of loveliness that you can pick up and stretch, bounce, wobble or swing like a rope. You want to be able to stretch it so thinly that you can see light through it. Please don't be tempted to add more flour unless you are panicking. Sticky is good. Err on the side of sticky rather than on the side of dry. Once you

have kneaded it, you pop it back into the mixing bowl to let it do its first rise. Unless this is called for, you don't need to grease the bowl.

Can I over-knead?
It is almost impossible to destroy dough at this point, especially if you are kneading by hand (although one of my students who is a serious sportswoman did destroy her dough by over-kneading). If your dough suddenly begins to fall apart and look a bit like spongy cottage cheese, you have over-kneaded it and you have to throw it away and start again.

How do I add things?
If you would like to incorporate fruit, nuts, cheese, olives, sun-dried tomatoes, etc., knead the dough without them first, cover the dough and allow it to rest for 15 minutes, then add them in. Imagine how much your hands would hurt if you tried to knead dough with walnuts in it for 10 minutes, and what a black smeary mess you would get if you kneaded olives in for 10 minutes. Don't worry about the dough – it will recover. Fold the ingredients in gently to keep them whole, especially if they are fragile. Cover the dough once more and allow to rest according to the recipe.

Rising
You need to let dough rise at various stages that will always be laid out in the individual recipes. Typically, dough made with yeast rises a couple of times before it is baked to help achieve a light crumb in the desired shape. The first rise takes place in the bowl in which it was mixed and the following rises vary according to what you are baking. At a temperature of 20°C/68°F, the first rise takes about 2 hours and the second rise takes about 1 hour.

At any point, you can put your dough in the fridge to slow it down. At 5°C/41°F (the temperature of the average fridge), dough will take about 8 hours to double in size. So if you all of a sudden need to go out, don't worry – just cover the bowl with clingfilm/plastic wrap so it

does not dry out and pop it in the fridge until you are ready to use it.

There are a few things to know about rising. i) If dough significantly more than doubles in size during its final rise, it risks using up all the power in the yeast before it is baked and it may collapse when it gets into the oven. You know your dough has over-risen if it collapses before you put it in the oven; if the crust has come away from the crumb during baking leaving holes between the crust and the crumb; or if the top is mottled with little black, burned spots. If you spot that your dough has over-risen before you bake it, eg. if the top of the loaf is uneven and wobbly looking or it has completely collapsed, don't panic. Pull it out of the loaf pan (or off the baking sheet or out of the proofing basket) and knead a little bit more flour into it. Shape it again and put it back to rise. It will recover quickly, so keep an eye on it.
ii) If dough has not risen enough, it will split in the oven. It splits along the top where the pan meets the dough or along the bottom where the baking sheet meets the dough. Chalk it up to experience and be a bit more patient next time.

iii) The texture, flavour and digestibility of bread are nicer if the dough has taken longer to rise. The Real Bread Campaign advises that 'real bread' takes a minimum of 4 hours to make. As dough rises, the yeast is literally eating the flour, breaking it down and making it easier to digest. The longer the dough rises, the more broken down the flour gets. Natural yeast is less powerful than commercial yeast, which is why sourdough bread takes a long time to rise. As a result, the flour is very well broken down. Many people find they can digest sourdough bread more easily. You can mimic sourdough bread by putting your normal dough in the fridge to rise, thus stretching out the rising time.

Covering dough for rising

Whatever the bread is rising in (the bowl, loaf pan, on the baking sheet or in a proofing basket) you should cover it so it does not dry out. For bread in a bowl, pan or basket, the best thing to use is a clean shower hat – the cheap, transparent kind you get in hotels. Yes! They are elasticized so they don't let air in and they are gathered so you can puff them up to stop them sticking to the dough when it rises. If you don't have a shower hat, you can pop the pan or basket in a clean plastic bag, blow it up and seal it. If the dough is rising on a baking sheet, or in a roasting pan, cover it with a dry tea towel so that it does not stick. The recipes will guide you.

Pulling risen dough out of a bowl

When the dough has finished rising and you take it out of the bowl to start shaping it, take it out gently. The recipes will state whether you should take it out onto a floured or an unfloured surface. Either way, please don't 'knock it back'. The dough has lots of lovely air in it and in most cases you want to keep it that way. Some recipes call for the dough to be rolled flat with a rolling pin, in which case you don't need to be so gentle.

Shaping

How on earth do you get the dough from a blob in a bowl into the shape you want it to be? How do you get air bubbles? The answer is that shaping is hard and it takes practice, and these guidelines will help.

i) Dry dough is easier to shape. If you are getting frustrated, put flour on the counter or knead more flour into the dough to make it easier to handle. Over time, as your skill grows, you will need less flour and become more comfortable with a wetter dough.

ii) Cold dough is easier to shape. Try doing the first rise in the fridge and then taking it out to shape it. Just remember that your cold dough will take several hours to double in size during the second rise. Be patient otherwise you will bake it too early and it will crack. If you are making enriched bread (with lots of butter), it is always much easier to shape when it is cold.

iii) The recipes give you some guidance regarding how to shape your dough but there are plenty of ways to shape and there is no single right way. If you have a way that works for you please use it – and let me know.

You could, of course, put the risen blob from the bowl right in the oven and bake it. It would bake right through but it would not rise any more, it might collapse, and it would continue to be a blob – edible, but not exactly beautiful. The reason for this is because the surface of the dough, when it has completed its first rise, is soft and squashy and there is no longer any structure against which the carbon dioxide bubbles can push. Imagine a balloon with holes in it: you cannot blow it up very well.

If you want your blob to rise, you need to give it some structure, creating tension on the surface so the carbon dioxide has something to push against (think of that balloon again) while leaving the nice, soft, pillowy dough as intact as you can on the inside. If there is no structure, the loaf will not rise well and will come out like a brick.

Right: Shaping is really what makes your loaf yours. Every recipe in this book will explain how to shape the dough for that particular bread, but once you have gained confidence, you can experiment with any shape you like.

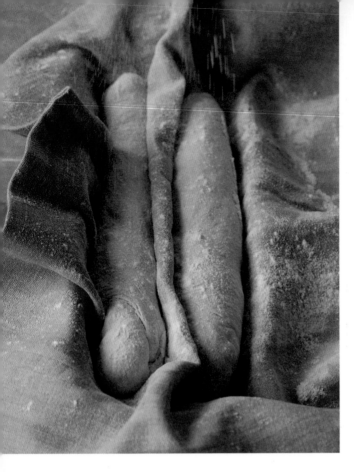

Regardless of the final shape, you frequently start by pulling the dough gently out of the bowl and onto the counter. At that point you do the 'stretch and fold'.

i) Pretend the blob of dough is a clock. Starting at noon, gently pinch about 1 cm/½ inch of the edge of the dough and pull it away from the blob, stretching it as far as you can without breaking it. Don't worry if you do, just try not to.

ii) Fold that pinched bit right back over the blob and gently lay it down. Repeat this action all round the blob of dough, essentially stacking it on itself. As you do it, you can turn the blob of dough, or move yourself around it. A scraper helps.

At this point you may be asked to make a loose or a tight ball, or a loose or a tight sausage.

To make a loose ball, simply flip the dough over so the folded bits are on the bottom and tuck the edges in all around the blob to make a ball.

To make a tight ball, flip the dough over as above. Then, place your hands gently on the dough and tuck the edges in firmly by moving your hands down the surface of the dough and right underneath it so that your little fingers actually touch underneath the dough, pinching some dough between them. Repeat this action, turning the dough blob after each tuck. You are effectively pulling the skin of the dough around itself. Once you have done it several times – and remember your little fingers should actually touch underneath the blob, pinching dough between them – your dough blob will look and feel like a big golf ball.

To make a loose sausage, simply roll the dough into a sausage shape after you have stretched and folded it and turn it seam side down, ready to rest for the next phase.

To make a tight sausage, roll the dough up after you have stretched and folded it but do it 'on the spot', gently stretching the dough toward you before each roll and tucking the dough into the roll with your fingers as you go. Think of trying to get a sleeping bag into a very small bag. Once you have done it should feel as firm as a foot stool. If it does not, turn it 90° so the short end is toward you, and try again. Once you are satisfied it is really firm, flip it over so it is seam side down and stretch the dough around each end by pulling the surface of the dough down and around the ends toward the table to seal them in.

After this, each recipe takes over, directing you how to deal with the dough to get the shape required. Of course, there are exceptions to the 'stretch and fold' starting point and they will be clearly indicated. You may, for example, be asked to pull the dough out and gently stretch it out or roll it out into a rectangle before stuffing it, or folding it up like a business letter ready for an envelope. You may also be asked to divide it into smaller pieces before shaping them into buns, rolls, or sausages.

I truly hope the shaping instructions are clear. If they are not, please let me know. However, be patient and be forgiving. They are not always easy to describe in words. If they are not clear, you can also watch the videos at **www.virtuousbread.com**

What can I proof and bake my bread in?

Once your bread is shaped, it has to do its second rise. To get a square loaf you need to shape the dough into a sausage and pop it in a loaf pan.

For something different, you can do the second rise in a flower pot, proofing basket, or even in a bowl lined with a floury tea towel.

If you want bread rolls or a freeform blob, you make the shapes and let them rise directly on a prepared baking sheet or roasting pan.

Pans, sheets, pans and flower pots can go right in the oven. If you are proofing in a bowl or a basket, however, you need to turn the dough out onto a prepared baking sheet to bake it. Individual recipes will direct you when there are alternative options for proofing and baking.

If you are baking in a pan or a flower pot remember to use a hard fat to grease the container. Oil does not work as well. If you are baking on a baking sheet, grease it, line it with non-stick parchment paper or sprinkle coarse cornmeal (polenta) or coarse semolina over it.

Baking

Times and temperatures are given with every recipe. Do get an oven thermometer to make sure your oven is doing what it should!

Before you pop your loaf in the oven, you may want to make a few slashes on its top with a sharp knife, blade or some scissors. You can do this for various reasons:
i) It reduces the risk of the bread splitting while it bakes.
ii) It increases the amount of crust by increasing the surface area of the bread.
iii) It makes a pretty pattern.

When is bread done?

Tap the bottom of the loaf. If it sounds hollow it is done, if it does not sound hollow it is not done. The bottom of the loaf should feel 'thin'

like a tambourine, not 'thick' like a tupperware full of mashed potatoes. Pop the loaf back in the oven for 5 minutes if it is not done yet.

You will learn, over time, how bread behaves in your oven. If your bread turns out to be a bit stodgy when it has cooled, pop it in the toaster, chalk it up to experience and bake it a bit longer next time. If you want to be technical, bread is baked when the inside of the loaf is 98°C/208°F. You can buy a special bread thermometer to test for temperature if you would like to.

Should I spray the oven?

Some bakers say 'yes' and some say 'no'. I don't know, I really don't. Try it and see. If you like the result of whatever you are doing, keep doing it and let us know.

What about fan-assisted/convection baking?

The fan-assisted/convection method bakes things faster and at different temperatures than normal baking. Further, fan-assisted seems to dry out the loaf while it is baking. Some fan-assisted ovens don't brown the bread at all and some brown it too quickly. If you don't have an option, please adjust the temperature and time according to your oven's manufacturer and experiment to get a result that pleases you.

When you remove your bread from the oven, remove it from the pan or baking sheet immediately and place it on a wire rack. Your bread needs air to circulate around it so that it cools properly.

Bread is still cooking as it cools so please resist the temptation to cut into it when it is hot – allow it to cool completely unless otherwise stated in the recipe.

Storing

Once cool, you can store bread in lots of different ways. I wrap it in a tea towel and put it in the bread container (mine is terracotta but others may be enamel or wood). I personally don't wrap bread in plastic or put it in the fridge but I know plenty of people who do both. Again, do whatever works for you.

18 Basic steps for the simplest bread

Basic steps for the simplest bread

If you can't wait to get baking and you want to know how to make the simplest loaf of bread, right now, here is how!

300 g/2⅓ cups strong wheat (bread) flour (white, wholemeal/whole-wheat or a mixture)

1.5 g/¾ teaspoon instant yeast, 3 g/1 teaspoon dried yeast, or 6 g/⅛ fresh yeast

200 g/¾ cup plus 2 tablespoons water

6 g/1½ teaspoons salt

small loaf pan, greased

MAKES 1 SMALL LOAF

Step One: if using instant or fresh yeast
Put all the ingredients in a big bowl and mix them together. [2]

Step One: if using dry yeast
Put the flour into a big bowl and make a well. Sprinkle the yeast in the well and add 100 g/½ cup of the water. Cover and allow to rest for 15 minutes. [1]

You may or may not get a beige sludge on top of the water, but don't worry – what is important is to dissolve the yeast. Add the rest of the ingredients and mix. [2]

Step Two
Knead well for 10 minutes – see page 12 for instructions. [3]

Step Three
Pop the dough back in the bowl and cover it. See page 14 for instructions. [4]

Allow it to rest for 1–2 hours until doubled in size.

Step Four
Pull the dough out gently onto an unfloured surface. Shape it into a tight sausage. See page 16 for instructions. [5]

Pop the sausage in the greased loaf pan. [6]

Step Five
Cover the dough and allow it to rest for 1 hour until doubled in size. Preheat the oven to 200°C (400°F) Gas 6.

Step Six
Bake the loaf in the preheated oven for 45 minutes. Remove from the pan and tap the bottom of the loaf. If it sounds hollow, it is done. See page 17 for instructions.

Step Seven
When it is done, remove the bread from the pan and place it on a wire rack to cool. See page 17 for more details.

Demystifying sourdough

Baking bread using sourdough is not scary, difficult or exclusive. Think of sourdough as the fourth kind of yeast: it is simply a paste of flour and water in which natural yeast is trapped. Everybody made bread with a sourdough starter until the mid 1850s when scientists discovered how to cultivate yeast into something we could see and hold in our hands. You can bake any kind of bread using a sourdough starter, you just need to demystify it.

Terminology

There are many words used in sourdough baking whose meanings may not be obvious. As ever, there is no single way to make sourdough bread, nor are there any standard terms and conditions. To that extent, it is important to begin with a shared vocabulary, and here is one I prepared earlier. You may use different terminology and I hope you will be able to translate this.

Sourdough starter (or just 'starter')

The sourdough starter is the gloop that you refresh when you want to make sourdough bread. I keep my sourdough starters in the fridge in airtight containers where they go to sleep and are in no danger of dying. I pull them out when I want to bake and then put them back again after.

Refreshed sourdough

The refreshed sourdough is the fresh-smelling result of adding flour and water to the starter. How you refresh sourdough varies according to the type of starter you are refreshing and the type of bread you are making. See details below.

Predough

When there is an intermediate dough between refreshing the starter and making the final dough, it is called a 'predough'. Not all recipes call for a predough. If you have the time and inclination, and want to build the flavour of your bread, follow a recipe that calls for a predough. The longer you take to make your bread the stronger it will taste.

Final dough

The final mixture that is eventually baked.

Polite notices

i) Sourdough bread does not need to taste sour. The 'sour' in sourdough refers to the sour smell of the starter when it has been left unrefreshed for a while. Don't be alarmed if your starter stinks, nor if it has a liquid floating on top of it. Once you have refreshed it, you will notice it smells fresh. Because the term is a little confusing, many bakers refer to sourdough bread as wild yeast bread or natural yeast bread.

ii) A lot of bread that is sold as sourdough bread has commercial yeast added to it. That's fine – it's still sourdough bread, but it is not 'pure' sourdough bread. Adding commercial yeast allows the baker to control, more precisely, the timing and nature of the proofing (how long it takes to rise and how high it gets). If you are concerned, ask the baker.

The process of baking with sourdough is similar to that which is followed to bake with commercial yeast. There are, however, a few important differences.

i) **You can make your own sourdough starter.** Unless you have a lab you cannot make your own yeast. For instructions on how to make a sourdough starter, see below.

ii) **Sourdough can be stored indefinitely as long as it is stored properly.** Commercial yeast, on the other hand, has a shelf life. You can freeze your starter, dry your starter or simply put your starter in an airtight container in the fridge. It will always come back to life when you mix it with some flour and water. You do not need to feed it regularly. When you are not using it, store it properly and forget about it. When you want to use it, refresh it according to the recipe.

iii) **The amount of sourdough you need to make bread is different from the amount of commercial yeast you need.** The amount of sourdough starter you need depends on the base flour of the starter and the type of flour used to refresh the starter and make the final dough. Until you are familiar with your starter and how it behaves when you refresh it and bake with it, use a recipe.

iv) **Your sourdough must be awake (airy and fresh smelling) to make bread that rises.** To do that, you 'refresh' it by mixing some of the starter from the fridge with some flour and some water according to the recipe. It takes between 4 and 24 hours to refresh a dormant sourdough starter depending on when it was last refreshed. Fresh and instant yeast, on the other hand, do not need to be refreshed (or 'proofed', as it is called when you are using them) and active dry yeast normally does. The process for proofing active dry yeast takes between 10–15 minutes versus the 4–24 hours it takes to ready a dormant sourdough for baking: similar process, different time scale.

v) **Sourdough bread takes longer to rise.** You can make good bread at home with commercial yeast in about 4 hours. Your sourdough bread will take 8–18 hours to make. It is this enforced longer rise that makes sourdough easier to digest and stronger in flavour. Over the hours the dough rises, the yeast breaks down the flour which means that our bodies can process it more easily.

vi) **Sourdough dough has a sticky texture that may be unfamiliar.** This sticky texture does not come from the amount of water in the dough. There are plenty of kinds of bread you make with commercial yeast that are far wetter than sourdough dough. The stickiness comes from the fact that refreshed dough has the consistency of sticky goo. When you add sticky goo to a perfectly normal flour and water mixture, you get sticky dough.

vii) **Sourdough bread does not rise as much as bread made with commercial yeast.** Commercial yeast is simply more powerful. With commercial yeast you are always looking for your dough at least to double in size – at whatever stage. Sourdough bread will only rise by about 1.5 times before the yeast begins to lose its puff. The relative weakness of the yeast in a sourdough starter is one of the reasons that the dough may be wetter than you are used to: all else being equal, wetter dough rises faster and expands a bit more easily than dryer dough.

Tips for beginners
i) Use recipes. Start with the ones on pages 26–27 to get your head around how sourdough works and begin to see how you can make it work for you.
ii) Use loaf pans rather than proofing baskets to bake until you get an eye and a feel for the dough. A loaf pan is easier for these reasons:
   a) It physically contains wetter dough more effectively than anything else, which means you are more likely to get a loaf than a blob.
   b) If it is greased, the dough will never stick and the loaf will come out in a regular shape (no bulging, no flat pancakes).
   c) It is easier to tell if dough is ready for the oven when it rises in a pan.
iii) Always use plastic (ie. clingfilm/plastic wrap, a bag or a shower hat) when covering sourdough at every stage. Resting times are long

and you don't want it to dry out (see page 14).
iv) Don't be afraid to make a mistake. Bread is forgiving and the ingredients are cheap. If your loaf is ugly you won't win a prize, but you can still toast it, and sourdough toast is particularly yummy.

Making your own RYE sourdough starter
Day One
Mix 25 g/3 tablespoons rye flour and 50 g/ 3½ tablespoons water together in a big bowl. Cover and leave on the counter for 24 hours.

Day Two
Add 25 g/3 tablespoons rye flour and 50 g/ 3½ tablespoons water to the mix. Stir and cover. Leave for 24 hours.

Day Three
Repeat as Day Two.

Day Four
Repeat as Day Two.

Day Five
Your starter should be bubbly. Congratulations! If your starter is not bubbly by the morning of Day Five, don't add any more flour, just cover it and let it sit for another 24 hours. If nothing has happened by then, your house could be too clean. Seriously! Stop using bleach or other antiseptic sprays on every surface. Revert to hot, soapy water to clean surfaces. You need germs and so does your sourdough!

Making your own WHEAT sourdough starter
Day One
Mix 50 g/6 tablespoons white or wholemeal/ wholewheat flour and 50 g/3½ tablespoons water together in a big bowl. Cover and leave on the counter for 24 hours.

Day Two
Add 50 g/6 tablespoons white or wholemeal/ wholewheat flour and 50 g/3½ tablespoons

warm water to the mix. Stir and cover. Leave for 24 hours.

Day Three
Repeat as Day Two.

Day Four
Repeat as Day Two.

Day Five
Your starter should be bubbly. Congratulations! If your starter is not bubbly by the morning of Day Five, don't add any more flour, just cover it and let it sit for another 24 hours. If nothing has happened by then, your house could be too clean. Seriously! Stop using bleach or other antiseptic sprays on every surface. Revert to hot, soapy water to clean surfaces. You need germs and so does your sourdough!

Storing your sourdough starter
If you don't want to bake straightaway and would prefer to store your starter at first, put it in the fridge in a big plastic container with an airtight lid, or in a kilner jar (the kind with the rubber seal and the clip). Whatever you use, make sure it is big because your starter will continue to froth up for a day or 2 before it calms down. Do not use a regular jam jar to store your starter at this point because it may explode.

After a couple of days in the fridge, your new starter will calm down. After a while, your starter will separate, dark liquid will float on the top and it will smell. Unless it is mouldy, all this is perfectly fine. I once found some starter in the back of the fridge that had been there for about 5 years. It was perfectly fine and refreshed beautifully.

You will only kill your starter if you leave it in a liquid state at room temperature for too long without feeding it. When it is cold, frozen or dried, it simply goes to sleep and does not need food. When it is sitting at room temperature, the yeast eventually dies and the starter goes mouldy. At that point, it is best to throw it away.

If you run out or if you kill it, it is not the end of the world. You can make more in 5 days. It is not like running out of yeast. If that happens, you have to find a store and buy more.

Using your sourdough starter

You refresh the starter when you need it. To do this, simply follow the instructions on the recipe you are using. Remember, 2 things:

i) You don't want to run out of starter because if you do, you have to make another one and that takes 5 days.

ii) You don't want to have a starter that is part wheat and part rye, or part rye and part spelt, because the grains perform differently and a mixed starter will make it difficult to follow recipes. That should not deter you from experimenting, but you may want some 'pure' starter as well to make your life a little easier (although possibly less fun).

To that end, you may want a reserve pot at the back of the fridge that you label 'sourdough starter, don't throw away'.

Making more starter

Rye

If you are concerned that you may run out, scrape the starter in the fridge into a bowl and weigh it. Add 3 times as much rye flour and 6 times as much water. Stir, cover and leave on the counter for 8–12 hours. It will bubble up, at which point you pop it into an airtight container and put it in the fridge. Voilà.

Wheat

If you are concerned that you may run out, scrape the starter in the fridge into a bowl and weigh it. Add the same amount of wheat flour and the same amount of water. Stir, cover and leave on the counter for 8–12 hours. It will bubble up, at which point you pop it into an airtight container and put it in the fridge. Voilà.

How do I use sourdough rather than yeast?

Explaining how to substitute a wheat sourdough starter and a rye sourdough starter for yeast requires more room then I have here. So, I have elected to explain how to substitute a rye sourdough starter for the yeast in any of the recipes in this or any other book. Once again, there are an infinite number of ways to do this and this is only one way. It always works for me.

Day One

i) Pick the recipe you would like to bake, note the amount of fresh yeast that is called for and double it to get the amount of rye sourdough starter you need. Weigh this out in a bowl.

ii) Take 25% of the flour that is called for in the recipe and put that in the bowl too.

iii) Take half as much water as you took of flour and put that in the bowl. So if you used 300 g/ 2⅓ cups flour, add 150 g/1⅛ cups water. Mush it all together with your hands, cover it and leave it overnight or all day on the counter. Write down how much flour and water you used because you will need to subtract that from the total amount called for in the recipe and use the balance the next day. If you are making an enriched dough, use milk instead of water if it is called for.

Day Two

The bowl will be full of a puffy, refreshed sourdough. Add the remaining flour and water that you need. Add all the other ingredients and knead well for 10 minutes. Pop the dough back in the bowl.

If you are making an enriched dough, you will need to follow a slightly different procedure – you will need to add the rest of the flour and milk in a 2-stage process:

i) In a separate bowl, measure the remaining flour that you need and make a well in it. Shred the puffy refreshed sourdough into the well, add the sugar and add the remainder of the liquid that is called for. Flick some flour on the well to close it and allow it to rest for 2 hours.

ii) Follow the kneading instructions given in the recipe – they will differ depending on what you are baking.

For both enriched and non-enriched recipes, rest the dough for twice as long as the recipe says at every stage. If the kitchen is cold, it may take 3 times longer at every stage. Remember, don't expect your sourdough to double, just to increase by around 1.5 times at every stage.

Preheat the oven to 230°C (450°F) Gas 8. Bake the sourdough bread for 10 minutes, then lower the temperature to 200°C (400°F) Gas 6 and bake for a further 30 minutes (for loaves) or 10 minutes (for buns).

Mixed loaf
using rye sourdough starter

Day One: refreshing the starter

10 g/⅓ oz. rye sourdough starter from the fridge

60 g/scant ½ cup wheat flour (white, wholemeal/whole-wheat or a mixture)

30 g/2 tablespoons water

Mix these ingredients together to refresh your rye sourdough starter. It will be a thick paste that you have to work together with your hands. Cover and leave on the counter for 8–12 hours. This makes 100 g/3½ oz. refreshed sourdough.

Day Two: making the dough

300 g/2⅓ cups wheat flour (white, wholemeal/whole-wheat or a mixture)

200 g/¾ cup water

5 g/1¼ teaspoons salt

Mix these ingredients with the refreshed sourdough from Day One and knead well for 10 minutes – see page 12 for instructions on kneading, adding more water if necessary to get a soft, stretchy dough that is the texture of your favourite pillow. Pop it back in the bowl, cover tightly and allow to rest for 1 hour.

Rising

Pretend the blob of dough in the bowl is a clock. Starting at noon, gently pinch about 1 cm/½ inch of the edge of the dough and pull it up and out, stretching it as far as you can without breaking it. Don't worry if you do, just try not to. Fold that pinched bit over the blob of dough and gently lay it down. Repeat this action all round the blob of dough. Once you have worked all around the blob, cover it tightly again and allow to rest for 1 hour.

Stretch and fold the dough in the bowl once more as if it were a clock. Cover again and allow to rest for 1 hour.

Repeat the clock method for the last time and rest for 1 hour again.

If you cannot be bothered to do all the stretching and folding, cover the bowl tightly and allow the dough to rest for 3 hours. The stretching and folding simply gives the dough extra puff.

Shaping

Pull the dough out gently onto an unfloured surface. Don't flour it unless you get frustrated. Shape the dough into a tight sausage according to the instructions on page 16 and pop it in a proofing basket or a loaf pan to rise. Cover it – using a shower hat, or popping it into a plastic bag which you then blow up to keep the plastic off the surface of the dough is best to keep the dough from drying out during the long rising time. Allow it to rise until it has grown in size 1.5 times, and an indentation made with your finger comes out completely in a minute or so. This will take 2–3 hours depending on the heat in the kitchen.

Preheat the oven to 230°C (450°F) Gas 8.

If you are baking in a loaf pan, pop it in the oven. If you have proofed the dough in a basket, gently turn out the dough onto a prepared baking sheet – see page 17 for instructions.

Bake the sourdough bread in the preheated oven for 10 minutes, then lower the temperature to 200°C (400°F) Gas 6 and bake for a further 30 minutes. It will sound hollow when it is done. Allow to cool completely on a wire rack.

Virtuous bread
using wheat sourdough starter

Day One: refreshing the starter

90 g/3 oz. wheat sourdough starter from the fridge

90 g/⅔ cup wheat flour (white, wholemeal/
whole-wheat or a mixture)

90 g/⅓ cup water

Mix these ingredients together to refresh your
wheat sourdough starter. Cover and leave on the
counter for 8–12 hours.

Day Two: making a predough

300 g/2⅓ cups wheat flour(white, wholemeal/
whole-wheat or a mixture)

200 g/¾ cup water

Measure 100 g/3½ oz. of the refreshed
sourdough back into the vat in the fridge and
leave the rest in your bowl. Add the flour and
water to the bowl to make a predough. Cover
and leave on the counter for 8–12 hours.

Day Three: making the dough

100 g/¾ cup wheat flour (white, wholemeal/
whole-wheat or a mixture)

10 g/2½ teaspoons salt

2 tablespoons lard (or butter)

2 tablespoons honey

Mix these ingredients with the predough from
Day Two and knead well for 10–15 minutes –
see page 12 for instructions on kneading, adding
more water if necessary to get a soft, stretchy
dough that is the texture of your favourite
pillow. Pop it back in the bowl, cover tightly
and allow to rest for 1 hour.

Rising

Pretend the blob of dough in the bowl is a clock.
Starting at noon, gently pinch about 1 cm/½ inch
of the edge of the dough and pull it up and out,
stretching it as far as you can without breaking

it. Don't worry if you do, just try not to. Fold
that pinched bit over the blob of dough and
gently lay it down. Repeat this action all round
the blob of dough. Once you have worked all
around the blob, cover it tightly again and allow
to rest for 1 hour.

Stretch and fold the dough in the bowl once
more as if it were a clock. Cover again and allow
to rest for 1 hour.

Repeat the clock method for the last time and
rest for 1 hour again.

If you cannot be bothered to do all the
stretching and folding, cover the bowl tightly and
allow the dough to rest for 3 hours. The stretching
and folding simply gives the dough extra puff.

Shaping

Pull the dough out gently onto an unfloured
surface. Don't flour it unless you get frustrated.
Shape the dough into a tight sausage according
to the instructions on page 16 and pop it in a
proofing basket or a loaf pan to rise. Cover it –
using a shower hat, or popping it into a plastic
bag which you then blow up to keep the plastic
off the surface of the dough is best to keep the
dough from drying out during the long rising
time. Allow it to rise until it has grown in size
1.5 times, and an indentation made with your
finger comes out completely in a minute or so.
This will take 4–6 hours depending on the heat
in the kitchen.

Preheat the oven to 230°C (450°F) Gas 8.

If you are baking in a loaf pan, pop it in the
oven. If you have proofed the dough in a basket,
gently turn out the dough onto a prepared
baking sheet – see page 17 for instructions.

Bake the sourdough bread in the preheated
oven for 10 minutes, then lower the temperature
to 200°C (400°F) Gas 6 and bake for a further
30 minutes. It will sound hollow when it is done.
Allow to cool completely on a wire rack.

everyday bread

For many people around the world, a meal is not a meal without bread. The father of a friend of mine simply won't sit down if there is no bread on the table. Another friend of mine can eat as much roast meat, stew, soup or lasagne as he likes but does not feel satisfied unless he has had bread. Eaten for breakfast with savoury or sweet things (or both), as sandwiches for lunch or dinner depending on where you are from, or as a plain companion to a highly flavoured or rich meal, bread is everywhere, all the time! Good-quality bread is a healthy and inexpensive way to fill up and can be just as much of a treat as cake when served with good butter and a smear of jam or honey. We should be thankful for our daily bread and make it out of the best ingredients that we can afford, to ensure that it is both flavoursome and nutritious.

300 g/2⅓ cups strong wholemeal/whole-wheat (bread) flour (or strong white bread flour if you prefer)

1.5 g/¾ teaspoon instant yeast, 3 g/1 teaspoon dry yeast, or 6 g/⅜ cake fresh yeast

200 g/¾ cup plus 2 tablespoons water

6 g/1½ teaspoons salt

prepared baking sheet (see page 17)

MAKES 1 BIG COB OR 4 SMALL ONES

brown cob

A cob can be large, for slicing and sharing, or small, for eating all on one's own. It is not a bap or a roll or a bun – it is a cob and it is common in central and northern England. 'Cob' is the Anglo-Saxon word for 'head' and may be where the bread gets its name. Some people, however, think it is because cobs look like cobblestones. It's a mystery and if you have any light to shed on it, please let me know! What is great about making a cob (big or small) is that you don't need a loaf pan or a proofing basket. All you need is a baking sheet.

If you are using instant or fresh yeast, put all the ingredients in a big bowl and mix them together. Tip out onto the counter and knead well for 10 minutes – see page 12 for instructions on kneading.

If you are using dry yeast, put the flour in a big bowl and make a well. Sprinkle the dry yeast in the well and add 100 g/½ cup of the water. Cover and allow to rest for 15 minutes. You may or may not get a beige sludge on the top of the water, but don't worry – what is important is to dissolve the yeast. Add the rest of the ingredients and mix. Tip out onto the counter and knead well for 10 minutes – see page 12 for instructions on kneading.

Pop the kneaded dough back into the bowl and cover with a tea towel, shower hat or plastic bag (see page 14). Allow to rest for 1–2 hours until doubled in size.

Pull the dough out onto an unfloured surface.

Shaping

Pretend your blob of dough is a clock. Starting at noon, gently pinch about 1 cm/½ inch of the edge of the dough and pull it up and out, stretching it as far as you can without breaking it. Don't worry if you do, just try not to. Fold that pinched bit over the blob of dough and gently lay it down. Repeat this action all round the blob of dough. As you do it, you can turn the blob of dough, or move yourself around it. Once you have worked all around the blob, use a scraper or a spatula to get underneath it and flip it over so the folds are now on the table and the smooth surface of the dough is on top.

Place both hands gently on top of the little blob and then bring them together underneath the dough (see photo, left), keeping them in contact with the dough the whole time, to stretch the skin of the dough around itself, creating surface tension so the dough can rise well. Repeat this action, turning the dough each time on the table as you do. You actually drag the dough around on the surface of the table to help you stretch the skin of the dough around itself. Do this as many times as you need to in order to get a really tight ball of dough that is perfectly round.

Using a scraper or spatula, pick up the ball of dough and transfer to the prepared baking sheet. Flour the top, cover with a dry tea towel and allow to rise for 45 minutes–1 hour until doubled in size.

Preheat the oven to 200°C (400°F) Gas 6.

Make a few slashes in the top of the cob with a sharp knife or scissors, if you like, and dust with a little more flour. Bake in the preheated oven for about 45 minutes. To check whether it is done, tap the bottom of the loaf. If it sounds hollow, it is done. If not, pop it back for another 5 minutes or so, until it does. Remove from the oven and transfer to a wire rack.

Variation: To make small cobs, divide the dough into 4 and repeat exactly as above, but space them 5–7 cm/2–3 inches apart on the baking sheet and bake in an oven preheated to 220°C (425°F) Gas 7 for 15–20 minutes.

soda bread

Soda bread, soda farls, wheaten bread, and brown soda bread refer to the same style of bread and are all eaten daily in both Northern Ireland and the Republic of Ireland. Simple and economical to make, they are loaves you can knock up in less than an hour when you have unexpected guests, when you want some lovely warm bread with your meal, or when you have some milk that has gone sour in the fridge. Baked either freeform or in a baking pan, this bread is fantastic eaten plain on the day it was made (especially with a green salad tossed in a sharp dressing), great toasted on day two and ready for the birds by day three. It's not a good keeper, but it always gets eaten really quickly!

450 g/3¼ cups wheat flour (plain/all-purpose white, wholemeal/whole-wheat, or a mixture)

1 teaspoon bicarbonate of soda/baking soda

2 g/½ teaspoon salt

400 ml/1⅔ cups buttermilk, sour milk or 50% plain yogurt and 50% full-fat milk (you can sour milk with lemon juice if you do not have sour milk, yogurt, or buttermilk, but if you do, add 1 teaspoon cream of tartar otherwise the bread will not rise very much)

optional extras: a handful or two of strong cheese either grated or crumbled, or mixed seeds, or dried fruit like raisins or dates or apricots, or nuts like walnuts or hazelnuts

prepared baking sheet (see page 17)

MAKES 1 BIG LOAF

Preheat the oven to 230°C (450°F) Gas 8.

Sift the flour, bicarbonate of soda/baking soda and salt into a bowl and mix very well. Add any optional extras at this point and mix in.

Add the buttermilk, sour milk or yogurt-milk and mix in well. You may have to resort to your hands in order to incorporate everything evenly but don't knead or squash – treat this dough lightly and the bread will be light. Turn the dough out onto a floured counter.

Shaping

Give the dough a light little knead just to bring it all together, give it some smoothness, and shape it into a ball. Wet your hands with a bit of water if you have to in order to minimize the sticking. Pick the ball up with a scraper and put it on the prepared baking sheet. Flatten it slightly so that it is about 4 cm/1½ inches high. Wet a knife or scraper and cut an 'X' into the ball nearly down to the bottom of the dough. The dough is so thick that if you do not cut an 'X' into it, the inside will not bake. Bake in the preheated oven for 10 minutes, then lower the oven temperature to 200°C (400°F) Gas 6 and bake for another 15–20 minutes. Remove from the oven and transfer to a wire rack.

To make a square loaf, spoon the dough into a small, well-greased baking pan. Wet the end of a wooden spoon and make a 2.5-cm/1-inch channel down the middle of the dough lengthwise. Bake as above.

To make soda farls, turn the dough out of the bowl onto a well floured counter. Sprinkle more flour over the top and give it a little knead. Flatten it gently with a floured rolling pin until 1 cm/⅜ inch thick. Cut the dough into wedges or squares or use a cookie cutter to stamp out rounds. Fry the farls in a very hot pan greased with oil or lard. Butter will burn so it's best not to use it, or use it in combination with another oil. The farls will rise up when they cook and when they do, flip them over to cook the other side. Wow – yum!

potato and rosemary bread

Leftover mashed potatoes make excellent bread – moist, soft, chewy and full of the flavour of the mash. Use whatever leftover mash you have, whether you make it with cream and butter, salt and pepper, mustard, horseradish, wasabi, anything at all. In this recipe I have added rosemary because it gives the bread colour and extra flavour.

If you are using instant or fresh yeast, put all the ingredients (except the mashed potatoes) in a big bowl and mix them together. Tip them out onto the counter and knead well for 10 minutes – see page 12 for instructions on kneading.

If you are using dry yeast, put the flour in a big bowl and make a well. Sprinkle the dry yeast in the well and add 100 g/½ cup of the water. Cover and allow to rest for 15 minutes. You may or may not get a beige sludge on the top of the water, but don't worry – what is important is to dissolve the yeast. Add the remaining ingredients (except the mashed potatoes) and mix. Tip out onto the counter and knead well for 10 minutes – see page 12 for instructions on kneading.

Pop the dough back into the bowl, cover with a dry tea towel and allow to rest for 15 minutes.

Pull the dough out of the bowl and gently fold in the potatoes until well incorporated but not completely blended in. The dough will get sticky and slack but use a scraper to gather it all up and get it off your hands and keep going. Don't add more flour unless you freak out and then please be sparing. This will make brilliant bread. Pop back in the bowl, cover again and allow to rest for 1–2 hours until doubled in size.

Pull the dough out onto a floured surface.

1 kg/8 cups strong white (bread) flour

5 g/2½ teaspoons instant yeast, 10 g/3¼ teaspoons dry yeast, or 20 g/1¼ cakes fresh yeast

500 g/2 cups water

20 g/1½ tablespoons salt

3–4 tablespoons fresh rosemary needles (or other fresh herb of your choice)

mashed potatoes – up to about half the volume of the dough

prepared baking sheet (see page 17)

MAKES 4 LOAVES

Shaping

Divide the dough into 4 equal portions. Flour your hands and shape each portion into a ball or sausage as best you can. Don't stretch and fold it as you would normally to form a skin and trap the air bubbles – the dough is too soft for this and it will sink a bit. Place on the prepared baking sheet, flour the tops, cover with a dry tea towel and allow to rest for 1 hour.

Preheat the oven to 200°C (400°F) Gas 6.

Make a few slashes in the tops of the loaves with a sharp knife or scissors, if you like, and dust with flour. Bake in the preheated oven for about 45 minutes. Remove from the oven and transfer to a wire rack.

Gram for gram, potatoes are usually cheaper than wheat. In Ireland they have been the staple food for generations and they would have made a proud filler for bread dough, stretching the expensive wheat flour further and doubling the size of the loaf for very little extra money. You can use any starchy vegetable in the same way and for the same reasons, eg. cooked sweet potato, yam, turnip, cassava root, pumpkin, or squash.

baguettes

The problem with putting a recipe for baguettes in any book is that it is so hard to achieve the baguette of our imaginations. We can achieve the shape, but the texture and taste of the final product may well disappoint. To make a really amazing baguette – the kind we remember from holidays and wonderful cafés – we need a particular kind of flour and we need a particular oven – one in which the heat source is close to the surface of the dough all the way around. A domestic oven just does not do this. Please don't let this put you off. Shaping baguettes is fun and the end result is always impressive. Just don't beat yourself up if they don't taste like they do when you buy them from a French bakery or eat them in a lovely bistro.

I like baguettes that are moist and chewy inside and have a certain acidity to them. To that end, I always make some of the dough the day before. To get lots of holes in your baguettes, you have to handle the dough frequently and gently, letting it rise several times in between. It takes patience and, for the beginner, a trusty egg timer. Try this out on a rainy day when you have nothing better to do, and see what you think. Better yet, tell us and send photos!

600 g/4⅔ cups plain/
all-purpose white wheat flour

400 g/1⅔ cups water

3 g/1½ teaspoons instant yeast,
6 g/2 teaspoons dry yeast, or
12 g/¾ cake fresh yeast

12 g/1 tablespoon salt

baguette proofing pan(s)
with capacity for 4 baguettes,
greased, or a roasting pan,
plenty of tea towels and
a prepared baking sheet
(see page 17)

MAKES 4

There is a strict definition of what it is to be a baguette in France. It must weigh between 240 g/8½ oz. and 310 g/11 oz., be between 55 cm/ 21½ inches and 70 cm/27½ inches long and have 7 cuts on the top. Every year the French Bakers' Union holds a competition to see who can make the best baguette in Paris. Although all the bakers live in Paris, many were not born in France and come from as far away as Cambodia, Vietnam and Senegal – former French colonies that have never lost their tradition of fine French bread.

Day One: making a predough

Put in a bowl: 200 g/1⅓ cups of the flour, 200 g/⅔ cup of the water and 1 g/½ teaspoon of the instant yeast OR 2 g/¾ teaspoon of the dry yeast OR 4 g/¼ cake of the fresh yeast. Mix, then cover with a clingfilm/ plastic wrap and allow to rest for 12–24 hours.

Day Two: making the dough

If you are using instant or fresh yeast, put the remaining 400 g/3⅓ cups flour, the remaining 200 g/1 cup water, the remaining 2 g/1 teaspoon instant OR 8 g/½ cake fresh yeast and all the salt in a big bowl. Add the predough from Day One. Mix the ingredients together, then scrape them onto the counter.

If you are using dry yeast, put the remaining 400 g/3⅓ cups flour in a big bowl and make a well. Sprinkle the remaining 4 g/1¼ teaspoons dry yeast in the well and add 100 g/scant ½ cup of the water. Allow to rest for 15 minutes. You may or may not get a beige sludge on the top of the water, but don't worry – what is important is

to dissolve the yeast. Add the remaining water, all the salt, and the predough from Day One. Mix the ingredients together, then scrape them onto the counter.

Knead well for 10–15 minutes – see page 12 for instructions on kneading – adding water by hand to keep the dough soft and pillowy (I usually add at least another 50 g/3 tablespoons but it is up to you). If your hands get sticky, just live with it! Under no circumstances should you add more flour at this point.

Pop the kneaded dough back into the bowl and cover with dry tea towel. Allow to rest for 30 minutes.

With the dough still in the bowl, pretend the blob of dough is a clock. Starting at noon, gently pinch about 1 cm/½ inch of the edge of the dough and pull it up and out, stretching it as far as you can without breaking it. Don't worry if you do, just try not to. Fold that pinched bit over the blob of dough and gently lay it down. Repeat this action all round the blob of dough.

Cover again and allow to rest for 30 minutes.

Stretch and fold the dough this way once more in the bowl. Cover again and allow to rest for 30 minutes.

Pull the dough out onto an unfloured surface. Stretch and fold it once as you did in the bowl. [1]

Roll it into a loose sausage. [2]

Cover with a dry tea towel and allow to rest for 10 minutes.

Shaping

Divide the dough into 4 equal portions. [3]

Stretch and fold each portion and shape them all into loose balls. [4]

Cover with a dry tea towel and allow to rest for 15 minutes.

Stretch and fold each portion again and roll up into tight sausages. Cover and allow to rest for 5 minutes.

Meanwhile, either grease the baguette proofing pans, or heavily flour a tea towel and place it in a roasting pan with deep sides. Please make sure the tea towel comes well up the sides of the pan.

Pick up one sausage and move it away from you. Roll it toward you as follows:

i) start with your hands together in the middle of each sausage, thumbs completely touching;

ii) roll toward you as you move your wrists – not your hands – apart – so that the fingertips

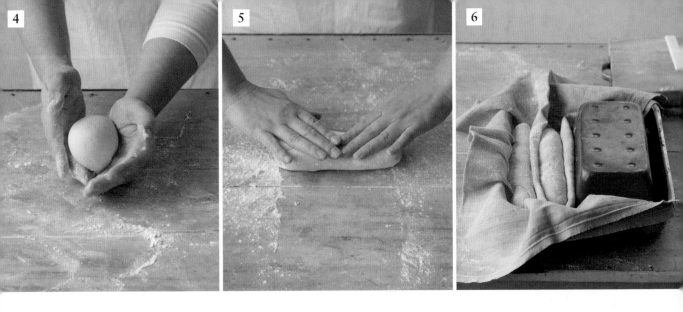

of the index finger of each hand meet and then the fingertips of the middle finger of each hand meet. As you do that, the palms of your hands travel effortlessly over the surface of the dough, stretching it out without applying any downward pressure. Once that has happened, you can move your hands apart as you roll; [5]

iii) pick up the dough, move it away from you and roll again as above. Do this as many times as you need to get the length you would like. Be aware that long baguettes are harder to handle than short ones, so if you are a novice, you may want to opt for shorter ones at first. Don't use any downward pressure, just gentle outward pressure. A true baguette is the same diameter from end to end and is not pointy.

Repeat with the rest of the sausages of dough.

Lay the baguettes one by one in the prepared proofing pan(s) or on the towel in the roasting pan, making sure there is a deep fold in the towel between each baguette so that they do not stick together as they rise. Remember, they will double in size! You may need to use a second towel as you go and that is fine. If you do not have enough baguettes to fill the roasting pan, wedge

them together with something like an upturned loaf pan or a book so they rise up and not out. [6]

Flour the tops of the baguettes, cover with a dry tea towel and allow to rest for 30–45 minutes or until doubled in size.

Preheat the oven to 230°C (450°F) Gas 8.

If you are using proofing pan(s), make slashes in the tops of the baguettes with a sharp knife or scissors and spray with fresh water from a plant sprayer to help achieve a crispy crust. Transfer the pan(s) to the oven.

If you proofed the dough on tea towels, gently pick up each baguette and lay it down on the prepared baking sheet. Don't be scared! They are more robust than you think. Make slashes in the tops of the baguettes with a sharp knife or scissors and spray with fresh water from a plant sprayer to help achieve a crispy crust. Transfer the sheet to the oven.

Bake the baguettes for about 15 minutes until golden brown. To check whether they are done, tap the bottoms of the baguettes. If they sound hollow, they are done. If not, pop them back for another 3–4 minutes or so. Remove from the oven and transfer to a wire rack.

pane di Genzano

This is sensational bread. It originates from Genzano, a little town outside of Rome, and is made extra special because of the dusting of bran than surrounds the bread. It also wobbles like a jelly before it is baked and that is rather fun too. Crispy on the outside and soft on the inside, this is great either fresh or toasted.

400 g/3¼ cups strong white (bread) flour

100 g/¾ cup strong wholemeal/whole-wheat (bread) flour

2.5 g/1¼ teaspoons instant yeast, 5 g/1½ teaspoons dry yeast, or 10 g/⅜ cake fresh yeast

380 g/1½ cups water

10 g/2½ teaspoons salt

bran, for dusting (either buy bran or simply sift some wholemeal/whole-wheat flour and use the bran that collects in the sieve/strainer)

23-cm/9-inch pie dish/plate, greased and dusted with bran

MAKES 1 LARGE LOAF

If you are using instant or fresh yeast, put all the ingredients in a big bowl and mix them together. Tip out onto the counter and knead well for 10 minutes – see page 12 for instructions on kneading. It will be liquid and sticky but persevere and do not add more flour. A scraper helps – push with your hands and scrape back with the scraper.

If you are using dry yeast, put the flour in a big bowl and make a well. Sprinkle the dry yeast in the well and add 100 g/½ cup of the water. Cover and allow to rest for 15 minutes. You may or may not get a beige sludge on the top of the water, but don't worry – what is important is to dissolve the yeast. Add the rest of the ingredients and mix. Tip out onto the counter and knead well for 10 minutes – see page 12 for instructions on kneading.

Pop the kneaded dough back into the bowl and cover with a tea towel, shower hat or plastic bag (see page 14). Allow to rest for 2 hours.

Lightly flour a board, your hands, and a dough scraper. Scrape the dough out onto the board. Shape the dough loosely into a round and pop it into the prepared pie dish/plate. Sprinkle the dough with bran. Cover and allow to rest for 1–2 hours until doubled in size. It will be wobbly when you jiggle it. Preheat the oven to 230°C (450°F) Gas 8.

Put the bread in the preheated oven and immediately lower the temperature to 200°C (400°F) Gas 6. Bake for 35 minutes. To check whether it is done, tap the bottom of the loaf. If it sounds hollow, it is done. If not, pop it back for another 5 minutes or so, until it does. Remove from the oven and transfer to a wire rack.

biovette

My friend Julia's mum, Anna del Conte, is Italian. She lives in England and is a national treasure due to the fantastic cookery books she has written. She dreams of 'biovette' which, she says, should puff open in the oven and be as light as air on the inside. It's the lard that does it. You can replace it with butter but the bun will not be as light.

500 g/4 cups plain/all-purpose white wheat flour

2.5 g/1¼ teaspoons instant yeast, 5 g/1½ teaspoons dry yeast, or 10 g/⅜ cake fresh yeast

250 g/1 cup water

1½ teaspoons malt syrup (if you can't find this, use honey)

30 g/2 tablespoons good-quality lard (or butter – see introduction above)

2½ tablespoons olive oil

10 g/2½ teaspoons salt

prepared baking sheet (see page 17)

MAKES 12

If you are using instant or fresh yeast, put all the ingredients in a big bowl and mix them together. Tip out onto the counter and knead well for 10 minutes – see page 12 for instructions on kneading.

If you are using dry yeast, put the flour in a big bowl and make a well. Sprinkle the dry yeast in the well and add 100 g/½ cup of the water. Cover and allow to rest for 15 minutes. You may or may not get a beige sludge on the top of the water, but don't worry – what is important is to dissolve the yeast. Add the rest of the ingredients and mix. Tip out onto the counter and knead well for 10 minutes – see page 12 for instructions on kneading.

Pop the kneaded dough back into the bowl and cover with a tea towel, shower hat or plastic bag (see page 14). Allow to rest for 2 hours until doubled in size.

Pull the dough out onto an unfloured surface.

Shaping
Divide the dough into 12 equal portions. Pretend each portion is a clock. Starting at noon, gently pinch about 1 cm/½ inch of the edge of the dough and pull it up and out, stretching it as far as you can without breaking it. Don't worry if you do, just try not to. Fold that pinched bit over the portion of dough and gently lay it down. Repeat this action all round the portion of dough. As you do it, you can turn the portion of dough, or move yourself around it. Roll into a loose ball, cover with a tea towel and allow to rest for 10 minutes.

Stretch and fold each portion again, as if it were a clock. Roll into a tight sausage, stretching the surface of the dough over itself to create tension without squeezing all the air out. Roll each sausage on the counter with both hands to make pointy ends. Your buns now look like slender lemons. With a very sharp knife or razor, cut a deep slash from end to end. Place the buns, slashed side down, on the prepared baking sheet. Dust with flour, cover with a dry tea towel and allow to rest for 1 hour or until doubled in size.

Preheat the oven to 220°C (425°F) Gas 7.

Turn the buns slashed side up again and if the slashes have closed up, use your knife to open them again gently. Bake in the preheated oven for 15–20 minutes. Remove from the oven and transfer to a wire rack.

farinata

I read about farinata years ago in a book about Sicily. The author described landing in Palermo and making his way immediately and without stopping to a tiny little café in the back streets where the best farinata was served. A piping-hot, bread-like substance made of chickpea flour and water was cut into strips and fried as a tasty snack. Later I came across a Ligurian chap who said, 'Fried? Farinata? Only the Sicilians would do that. They fry everything.' Ecco! So now, for vegetarians everywhere, for the gluten-intolerant and simply for gluttons who are not gluttons for punishment, a recipe for farinata that does not require frying and that was pronounced 'excellent' by three Italians: one from Rome, one from somewhere in Liguria, and a Sicilian who was most brave about the lack of oil. It has a curious texture, a little like stiff custard.

200 g/1½ cups chickpea flour (also known as gram flour)

640 ml/2⅔ cups water

4 g/1 teaspoon salt

optional extra: top with fresh or dried herbs before baking

23-cm/9-inch pie dish/plate, greased with olive oil

SERVES 8

Put the ingredients in a bowl and whisk with a balloon whisk to combine. Cover with clingfilm/plastic wrap and allow to rest for a good few hours, preferably overnight.

Preheat the oven to 220°C (425°F) Gas 7.

Whisk up the batter again and pour it in the prepared pie dish/plate. Bake in the preheated oven for 45–50 minutes or until golden and thoroughly set.

Eat it hot, warm or cold, cut in slices and served with a lovely green salad and a nice glass of wine. You can, of course, do as the Sicilians do and cut the cold farinata into strips and fry it. It is fantastic with fried eggs.

milk bread

Milk bread or morning bread has long been eaten all over the world. It was a way of using up milk (even sour milk) and a way of getting the valuable protein and vitamins from milk into the diet in a simple and more portable way! An all-in-one breakfast – milk and cereal in a solid form! How practical. Milk bread is delicious and the crumb and crust are soft and chewy. It is best made with full-fat milk and yummy when eaten with butter and jam.

300 g/2⅓ cups wheat flour (strong or plain/all-purpose white, wholemeal/whole-wheat, or a mixture)

1.5 g/¾ teaspoon instant yeast, 3 g/1 teaspoon dry yeast, or 6 g/⅜ cake fresh yeast

200 g/¾ cup plus 2 tablespoons milk, heated up to boiling point, then cooled to room temperature (see page 11)

6 g/1½ teaspoons salt

TO GLAZE

1 tablespoon honey

1 tablespoon milk

prepared baking sheet or small loaf pan, greased (see page 17)

**MAKES 8 BUNS OR
1 SMALL LOAF**

If you are using instant or fresh yeast, put all the ingredients in a big bowl and mix them together. Tip out onto the counter and knead well for 10 minutes – see page 12 for instructions on kneading.

If you are using dry yeast, put the flour in a big bowl and make a well. Sprinkle the dry yeast in the well and add 100 g/½ cup of the milk. Cover and allow to rest for 15 minutes. You may or may not get a beige sludge on the top of the water, but don't worry – what is important is to dissolve the yeast. Add the rest of the ingredients and mix. Tip out onto the counter and knead well for 10 minutes – see page 12 for instructions on kneading.

Pop the kneaded dough back into the bowl and cover with a tea towel, shower hat or plastic bag (see page 14). Allow to rest for 1–2 hours until doubled in size.

Pull the dough out onto an unfloured surface.

Shaping

Divide the dough into 8 equal portions and form into tight balls. Put on a floured tea towel, cover and allow to rest for 45 minutes. In the meantime, heat the honey and milk together, then allow to cool down.

Preheat the oven to 220°C (425°F) Gas 7.

Transfer the buns to the prepared baking sheet and brush with the milk and honey glaze. Bake in the preheated oven for 15–20 minutes until golden brown. Remove from the oven and transfer to a wire rack.

Variation: You can also bake this bread as a loaf in a small loaf pan.

graubrot

Germany is applying for recognition from UNESCO for being a place of 'intangible cultural heritage' for bread: there are more than 2,600 varieties. When my mother emigrated from Germany to Canada, she cried every day, longing for the bread from home. She baked all of our bread until a German bakery opened not so far away. There, she bought – and still buys – graubrot, so called because the rye content gives it a grey hue.

1 kg/8 cups rye flour (dark rye will make an earnest loaf, light rye will be a little lighter)

200 g/1½ cups strong wholemeal/whole-wheat (bread) flour

6 g/3 teaspoons instant yeast, 12 g/4 teaspoons dry yeast, or 24 g/1½ cakes fresh yeast

700 g/2¾ cups water

25 g/2 tablespoons salt

5 g/2 teaspoons ground coriander (optional)

15 g/1½ tablespoons cumin or caraway seeds (optional)

1 big loaf pan or 2 small loaf pans, well greased; or a prepared baking sheet (see page 17); or a big proofing basket or 2 smaller baskets, well floured, and a prepared baking sheet

MAKES 1 BIG LOAF OR 2 SMALL ONES

If you are using instant or fresh yeast, put all the ingredients in a big bowl and mix them together. Tip out onto the counter and knead well for 10 minutes – see page 12 for instructions on kneading.

If you are using dry yeast, put the flour in a big bowl and make a well. Sprinkle the dry yeast in the well and add 100 g/½ cup of the water. Cover and allow to rest for 15 minutes. You may or may not get a beige sludge on the top of the water, but don't worry – what is important is to dissolve the yeast. Add the rest of the ingredients and mix. Tip out onto the counter and knead well for 10 minutes – see page 12 for instructions on kneading.

Pop the kneaded dough back into the bowl and cover with a tea towel, shower hat or plastic bag (see page 14). Allow to rest for 1–2 hours until doubled in size.

Pull the dough out onto an unfloured surface.

Shaping
To use a big loaf pan, thoroughly wet your hands and gather the dough up into a ball. Pass the dough from hand to hand and smooth it into a brick in the shape of the pan. Place the dough in the prepared pan, making sure it comes only two-thirds up the side. To make 2 small loaves, divide the dough in 2, shape and place into smaller pans.

Alternatively, shape the dough into a brick as above and roll in plenty of flour. Place it gently in the prepared proofing basket, making sure it comes only two-thirds up the side. To make 2 small loaves, divide the dough in 2, shape and place into smaller proofing baskets. You can also use a shallow bowl(s) lined with floury tea towels.

Cover the dough with a damp tea towel, shower hat or plastic bag (see page 14) and allow to rise for about 45 minutes–1 hour until it has risen to the top of the pan/basket.

Preheat the oven to 200°C (400°F) Gas 6.

If you are rising the dough in a basket, gently tip it out onto the prepared baking sheet. Bake the bread in its pan or on the baking sheet in the preheated oven for about 45 minutes. To check whether it is done, tap the bottom of the loaf. If it sounds hollow, it is done. If not, pop it back for another 5 minutes or so, until it does. Remove from the oven and transfer to a wire rack.

basic rye

Rye grows well in cold, northern climates and is one of the grains of choice all over northern Europe and into Russia. Rye bread gets a bad rap because people think it dense, heavy and brick-like. In fact, this does not have to be true at all. Rye is much more absorbent than wheat, so it simply needs more water to make a good loaf. Rye bread not only tastes great, but it requires no kneading and it lasts for a good four to five days because it is so damp. In fact, don't bother cutting into it until two days after it is baked.

300 g/2⅓ cups light rye flour

1.5 g/¾ teaspoon instant yeast, 3 g/1 teaspoon dry yeast, or 6 g/⅛ cake fresh yeast

250 g/1 cup water

6 g/1½ teaspoons salt

optional extras: 1 teaspoon cumin, coriander, caraway, dill fennel or any other seeds of your choice, either mixed into the dough, sprinkled on the bottom of the loaf pan, or on top of the loaf before it goes in the oven

small loaf pan, greased

MAKES 1 SMALL LOAF

If you are using instant or fresh yeast, put all the ingredients (except the seeds) in a big bowl and mix them well to ensure the yeast and salt and completely integrated in the dough.

If you are using dry yeast, put the flour in a big bowl and make a well. Sprinkle the dry yeast in the well and add 100 g/½ cup of the water. Cover and allow to rest for 15 minutes. You may or may not get a beige sludge on the top of the water, but don't worry – what is important is to dissolve the yeast. Add the rest of the ingredients (except the seeds) and mix.

You don't have to knead this dough but stir it well to ensure the yeast and salt are evenly mixed in. It will be like stirring porridge or mud pies: satisfying and messy. Add more water if necessary to make a soft dough. It should not come away cleanly from the bowl, but be much softer – you should easily be able to press your fingers into it.

Shaping

Thoroughly wet your hands and gather the dough up into a ball. Pass the dough from hand to hand and smooth it into a brick shape. Place the dough in the prepared pan, making sure it comes only two-thirds up the side. Do not press it down into the corners, try to even it out or tidy it up; it will find its own level and the less you handle it, the lighter it will be. Cover the dough with a damp tea towel, clingfilm/plastic wrap or (best) a shower hat with plenty of head room. Allow to rise for 2–4 hours until it has risen to the top of the pan. There will be air bubbles on the surface.

Preheat the oven to 200°C (400°F) Gas 6.

Either dust the dough with flour and or spray the dough with water from a plant sprayer and sprinkle seeds of your choice on top. Bake in the preheated oven for 45 minutes. To check whether it is done, tap the bottom of the loaf. If it sounds hollow, it is done. If not, pop it back for another 5 minutes or so, until it does. Remove from the oven and transfer to a wire rack.

250 g/2 cups strong white (bread) flour

500 g/4 cups light rye flour (if you cannot get light rye flour, sift some dark rye flour and save the bran and germ in the sieve/strainer for putting on your cereal, and use the light rye flour in the bowl for the crackers)

3.5 g/1¾ teaspoons instant yeast, 7 g/2¼ teaspoons dry yeast, or 15 g/1 cake fresh yeast

500 g/2 cups whole milk (cold is fine)

10 g/2½ teaspoons salt

40 g/3 tablespoons honey

10 g/1 tablespoon ground anise (or cinnamon or cumin or coriander or ginger)

coarse sea salt, and caraway seeds, black and white sesame seeds, poppy seeds and/or dried herbs (don't use cheese, as it will burn!), to decorate

Swedish 'kruskavel' (textured rolling pin) (optional)

prepared baking sheets (see page 17)

MAKES 25–30

Swedish cracker bread

I had never really thought about where crackers come from. Even being a bread baker did not cause me to be curious. Maybe they were extruded in factories somewhere? I never really knew and yet I love crackers and have spent a lot of time in Sweden eating cracker bread. I associate it with picnics, celebrations, breakfast on the run, and I top it with thin slices of cheese, butter and jam, pickled herring and sour cream.

I asked my friend, Heléne Johansson, an incredible baker in Stockholm, for a recipe and, in her typical generous way, she gave me one which I have adapted only slightly. Be warned: it is labour-intensive to make crackers (all that rolling) but it may change your life and it is unlikely you will ever buy crackers again. Heléne owns and runs the Brunkebergs Bageri in Stockholm, Sweden.

Day One: making the dough

If you are using instant or fresh yeast, put all the ingredients in a big bowl and mix them together. Tip out onto the counter and knead well for 10 minutes – see page 12 for instructions on kneading. This dough is a bear to knead and it is easiest if you use a scraper to help you gather it all up. The honey coupled with the rye makes it tough, but persevere and you will be rewarded.

If you are using dry yeast, put the flours in a big bowl and make a well. Sprinkle the dry yeast in the well and add 100 g/½ cup of the milk. Cover and allow to rest for 15 minutes. You may or may not get a beige sludge on the top of the water, but don't worry – what is important is to dissolve the yeast. Add the rest of the ingredients and mix. Tip out onto the counter and knead well for 10 minutes – see page 12 for instructions on kneading.

Pop the dough back in the bowl, cover and allow to rest overnight.

Day Two: shaping and baking

Pull the dough out of the bowl and onto a floured surface. Divide into equal portions about the size of golf balls. [1]

Cover with a tea towel and allow to rest for 5 minutes.

Preheat the oven to 200°C (400°F) Gas 6.

On the well-floured surface, and with a well-floured rolling pin, roll each portion of dough out extremely thinly. Traditionally you roll them into a round and use a cutter to cut a hole out of the middle so you can store them by threading a string through them and hanging them up. However, it is also fun to roll them into ovals, squares, rectangles or wacky shapes.

Once you have rolled your shape, prick it liberally with a fork, roll it with a 'kruskavel' or thump it gently with a meat tenderizer – the dough needs indentations otherwise it will puff up in the oven. [2]

Spray the shapes with fresh water from a plant sprayer and decorate with a bit of coarse sea salt (be sparing, as there is salt in the dough) and your choice of toppings – take your pick to make them tasty and beautiful. [3]

Place the shapes on the prepared baking sheets, about 1 cm/½ inch apart. Bake in the preheated oven for 10–12 minutes. Watch them carefully, as they burn in an instant!

Remove from the oven and cool completely on a wire rack. Once the crackers are cold and completely crisp, you can store them almost indefinitely. If you live in a dry climate, hang them on strings! If not, pop them in an airtight tin.

If they are not completely crisp when they are all baked, or if they get a bit soggy, preheat the oven to 50°C (120°F) or its lowest setting, and put the crackers in. Turn the oven off, close the door and leave them there until the oven has cooled down. They will crisp up nicely.

Danish rye

Danish Rye is not strictly Danish! It is eaten all over northern and eastern Europe, getting its texture from the grains and seeds in the dough, and its colour and flavour from molasses. Its German cousin is pumpernickel and if you think you don't like it, please try this recipe. It was given to me by an amazing Swedish baker named Mattias Ljungberg who owns Tössebageriet, one of the oldest bakeries in Stockholm. When he and his father took over Tösse they found old books containing the original recipes. My heartfelt thanks to Mattias for sharing some of these with me. I have adapted this one slightly.

Day One: soaking
Put the kibbled/cracked rye and seeds in a bowl and cover with the cold water. Allow to soak overnight. It is very important that the water is cold, as warm water will sour the grains and give you tummy ache.

Day Two: making the dough
If you are using instant or fresh yeast, put the flours, yeast, salt, tepid water, molasses and the seeds and their soaking water in a big bowl and mix. Tip out onto the counter and knead well for 10 minutes – see page 12 for instructions on kneading.

If you are using dry yeast, put the flours in a big bowl and make a well. Sprinkle the dry yeast in the well and add the tepid water. Cover and allow to rest for 15 minutes. Add the salt, molasses and the seeds and their soaking water and mix. Tip out onto the counter and knead well for 10 minutes – see page 12 for instructions on kneading. The dough will look like a cross between baby poo and cake mixture, but don't let that put you off – it bakes beautifully.

Cover the dough with a tea towel, shower hat or plastic bag (see page 14) and allow to rest for 30 minutes.

Shaping
To use a big loaf pan, spoon the dough into the prepared pan, making sure it comes only two-thirds up the side. To use 2 small pans, divide the dough in 2 and spoon into the smaller pans. Cover the dough as above again. Allow to rise for 1–2 hours until it has risen to the top of the pan.

Preheat the oven to 240°C (475°F) Gas 9.

Put the loaf pan(s) in the preheated oven and immediately lower the temperature to 180°C (350°F) Gas 4. Bake for 45 minutes or until the bread has come away from the side of the pan. Remove from the pan and cool on a wire rack lined with a tea towel to prevent this soft bread from sinking into the rack. Let cool completely and do not even try to cut the bread until the next day.

90 g/⅔ cup kibbled/cracked/clipped/cut rye (available from healthfood stores or a miller. If you cannot get rye, you can normally find kibbled/cracked/clipped/cut wheat (bulghur) or spelt (farro). In a pinch you could use barley too which is widely available.)

75 g/½ cup mixed seeds (eg. sunflower, pumpkin, flax, sesame, poppy)

150 g/scant ⅔ cup cold water

200 g/1¼ cups light rye flour

100 g/¾ cup strong white (bread) flour

4.5 g/2¼ teaspoons instant yeast, 9 g/3 teaspoons dry yeast, or 18 g/1⅛ cakes fresh yeast

150 g/scant ⅔ cup tepid water

9 g/2¼ teaspoons salt (if you are using honey, increase the salt to 18 g/1¼ tablespoons)

110 g/scant ½ cup molasses/dark treacle

1 big loaf pan or 2 small loaf pans, well greased

MAKES 1 BIG LOAF OR 2 SMALL ONES

Russian rye

It's odd that coriander seeds – both whole and ground – are a traditional cooking and baking ingredient all over northern Europe and Russia when, until recently, the leaves and roots were not used at all. Where did all the seeds come from? Where did all the leaves go? They cannot all have simply stayed in Thailand. Maybe they did – do contact me if you have the answer.

I do know that the Hanseatic League – a trading league founded more than 1,000 years ago in Lübeck – spread the most exotic ingredients, eg. spices, coffee, tea, cocoa, dates, all over northern and eastern Europe, creating some common food traditions in vastly different cultures. Russian rye bread, therefore, is consumed in one form or another in many places. I probably had it for the first time, however, in the USSR in 1984 when bread was the best thing on the menu everywhere I went.

300 g/2⅓ cups dark or light rye flour

1.5 g/¾ teaspoon instant yeast, 3 g/1 teaspoon dry yeast, or 6 g/⅛ teaspoon fresh yeast

200 g/¾ cup water

3 g/¾ teaspoon salt

50 g/3 tablespoons molasses/ dark treacle or malt syrup (or a combination)

5 g/2½ teaspoons ground coriander

coriander seeds, to sprinkle

small loaf pan, greased

MAKES 1 SMALL LOAF

If you are using instant or fresh yeast, put all the ingredients (except the coriander seeds) in a big bowl and mix them together with a big wooden spoon.

If you are using dry yeast, put the flour in a big bowl and make a well. Sprinkle the dry yeast in the well and add 100 g/½ cup of the water. Cover and allow to rest for 15 minutes. You may or may not get a beige sludge on the top of the water, but don't worry – what is important is to dissolve the yeast. Add the rest of the ingredients (except the coriander seeds) and mix with a big wooden spoon.

The dough will be stiff and very sticky. You can use your hands but you may land up with most of the dough on your hands and very little in the bowl. You do not need to knead rye flour, as the gluten in it is weak and not stretchy, so kneading will not help it rise. Add more water for a soft dough, if necessary – you should easily be able to press your fingers into it and it should be the texture of a mud pie.

Shaping

Sprinkle some coriander seeds liberally over the base and sides of the loaf pan. Thoroughly wet your hands and gather the dough up into a ball. Pass the dough from hand to hand and smooth it into a brick in the shape of the pan. Place the dough in the prepared pan, making sure it comes only two-thirds up the side. Do not press it down into the corners, try to even it out or tidy it up; it will find its own level and the less you handle it, the lighter it will be. Cover the dough with a damp tea towel, clingfilm/plastic wrap or (best) a shower hat with plenty of head room. Allow to rise for about 2 hours until it has risen to the top of the pan. There will be air bubbles on the surface.

Preheat the oven to 200°C (400°F) Gas 6.

Spray the dough with fresh water from a plant sprayer and sprinkle more coriander seeds on top. Bake in the preheated oven for 45 minutes. Remove from the oven and transfer to a wire rack. Do not even try to cut the bread until the next day.

pita bread

Prevalent all over the Middle East and North Africa, these little pocket breads are now found all over the world, as people from these lands have moved around. Most supermarket varieties are industrially manufactured and so are full of additives and taste pretty lame. Some specialty shops have great pita but nothing beats the sense of wonder as you pull puffy pitas out of the oven.

Once out of the oven, immediately cut them open so they don't seal themselves shut and either eat them straightaway or tuck them in cloth napkins to keep them soft – they harden quickly otherwise. Once completely cool you can freeze them and simply toast them to revive them.

600 g/4¾ cups strong white (bread) or wholemeal/whole-wheat (bread) flour (you can substitute spelt or kamut flour)

3 g/1½ teaspoons instant yeast, 6 g/2 teaspoons dry yeast, or 12 g/¾ cake fresh yeast

360 g/1½ cups water

10 g/2½ teaspoons salt

prepared baking sheet (see page 17)

MAKES 8 BIG PITAS OR 12 SMALLER ONES

If you are using instant or fresh yeast, put all the ingredients in a big bowl and mix them together. Tip out onto the counter and knead well for 10 minutes – see page 12 for instructions on kneading.

If you are using dry yeast, put the flour in a big bowl and make a well. Sprinkle the dry yeast in the well and add 100 g/½ cup of the water. Cover and allow to rest for 15 minutes. You may or may not get a beige sludge on the top of the water, but don't worry – what is important is to dissolve the yeast. Add the rest of the ingredients and mix. Tip out onto the counter and knead well for 10 minutes – see page 12 for instructions on kneading.

Pop the kneaded dough back into the bowl and cover with a tea towel, shower hat or plastic bag (see page 14). Allow to rest for 1–2 hours until doubled in size.

Pull the dough out onto an unfloured surface.

Shaping
Pretend your dough is a clock. Starting at noon, gently pinch about 1 cm/½ inch of the edge of the dough and pull it up and out, stretching it as far as you can without breaking it. Don't worry if you do, just try not to. Fold that pinched bit over the portion of dough and gently lay it down. Repeat this action all round the portion of dough. As you do it, you can turn the portion of dough, or move yourself around it. Roll the dough into a tight sausage and cut it into 8–12 equal slices. Allow to rest under a tea towel for 5 minutes. Take each portion and stretch and fold as above, then roll into tight balls. Allow to rest under a dry tea towel for 5 minutes.

Flatten each ball on a floured surface into a disc no more than ½ cm/¼ inch thick using a rolling pin or your hands. Use a scraper or spatula to get the discs off the counter and place on the prepared baking sheets. Cover with a damp tea towel and allow to rest for 45 minutes.

Preheat the oven to 230°C (450°F) Gas 8.

Bake the pitas in the preheated oven for 8–10 minutes until puffed and just golden. Cut them open so they don't seal as they cool, but watch out for hot steam! Wrap in cloth napkins until ready to eat.

simit

Simit is eaten for breakfast all over Turkey. Hot out of the oven (either at home or from a local baker) it is eaten plain, with a cup of coffee, or with jam, yogurt or cheese.

400 g/3¼ cups strong white (bread) flour

2 g/1 teaspoon instant yeast, 4 g/1¼ teaspoons dry yeast, or 8 g/½ cake instant yeast

300 g/1¼ cups water

8 g/2 teaspoons salt

TO DECORATE

250 g/1 cup water

2 tablespoons molasses/ dark treacle

nigella and sesame seeds

prepared baking sheet (see page 17)

MAKES 12

If you are using instant or fresh yeast, put all the ingredients in a big bowl and mix them together. Tip out onto the counter and knead well for 10 minutes – see page 12 for instructions on kneading.

If you are using dry yeast, put the flour in a big bowl and make a well. Sprinkle the dry yeast in the well and add 100 g/½ cup of the water. Cover and allow to rest for 15 minutes. Add the rest of the ingredients and mix. Tip out onto the counter and knead well for 10 minutes – see page 12 for instructions on kneading.

Pop the kneaded dough back into the bowl and cover with a tea towel, shower hat or plastic bag (see page 14). Allow to rest for 1–2 hours until doubled in size. After this, pull the dough out onto an unfloured surface.

Shaping

Divide the dough into 12 equal portions and form into tight balls. Put on a floured tea towel, cover and allow to rest for 30 minutes.

Roll each ball into a 30-cm/12-inch long sausage. Twist a few times, bend into a ring and seal the ends well. Place on the baking sheets. [1]

Cover with the floured tea towel and allow to rest for 1 hour. To decorate, mix the water and molasses and pour into a wide, shallow bowl. Put the seeds on a plate. Dip each simit in the water, then the seeds. [2]

Make sure each simit is well coated with seeds. [3]

Gently cover with a tea towel and allow to rest for 30 minutes. Preheat the oven to 240°C (475°F) Gas 9. If the rings have closed up at all, stretch out again and allow to rest again for 15 minutes. If not, allow to rest for a total of 45 minutes. Bake in the preheated oven for 15 minutes.

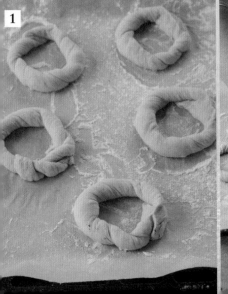

pide ekmeghi

The bakers of the Ottoman Empire believed that the Angel Gabriel taught Adam how to bake when he was expelled from the Garden of Eden. In Turkey and across the entire Muslim world, bread is considered holy – it is a blessing from God and it is a sin to waste it.

The Turks grow fantastic strong bread flour and have a vast array of delicious types of bread. Simple to make (indeed frequently still made fresh, two or even three times a day), pide ekmeghi is the bread you will find on the table of most Turkish people most days of the year. It is a perfect companion for hummus, feta cheese, honey, hard-boiled eggs or olives, or even butter and jam.

600 g/4/¾ cups strong white (bread) flour

3 g/1½ teaspoons instant yeast, 6 g/2 teaspoons dry yeast, or 12 g/¾ cake fresh yeast

400 g/1⅔ cups water

12 g/1 tablespoon salt

TO DECORATE

milk, or egg lightly beaten with 1 tablespoon water, to glaze

nigella and sesame seeds

prepared baking sheet (see page 17)

MAKES 2 LOAVES

If you are using instant or fresh yeast, put all the ingredients in a big bowl and mix them together. Tip out onto the counter and knead well for 10 minutes – see page 12 for instructions on kneading.

If you are using dry yeast, put the flour in a big bowl and make a well. Sprinkle the dry yeast in the well and add 100 g/½ cup of the water. Cover and allow to rest for 15 minutes. You may or may not get a beige sludge on the top of the water, but don't worry – what is important is to dissolve the yeast. Add the rest of the ingredients and mix. Tip out onto the counter and knead well for 10 minutes – see page 12 for instructions on kneading.

Pop the kneaded dough back into the bowl and cover with a tea towel, shower hat or plastic bag (see page 14). Allow to rest for 1–2 hours until doubled in size.

Pull the dough out onto an unfloured surface.

Shaping

Divide the dough into 2 equal portions. Pretend each portion is a clock. Starting at noon, gently pinch about 1 cm/½ inch of the edge of the dough and pull it up and out, stretching it as far as you can without breaking it. Don't worry if you do, just try not to. Fold that pinched bit over the portion of dough and gently lay it down. Repeat this action all round the portion of dough. As you do it, you can turn the portion of dough, or move yourself around it. Tuck it up into a loose ball. Cover with a tea towel and allow to rest for 30 minutes.

Gently stretch each ball into a disc shape about 2.5 cm/1 inch thick. Place on the prepared baking sheet. Cover with a tea towel and allow to rest again for 30 minutes.

Preheat the oven to 230°C (425°F) Gas 7.

Press your fingertips lightly into the surface of the dough to make little dimples. Not too hard! You just want to make the surface uneven. To decorate, brush the dough with either milk or the egg wash and sprinkle seeds over the top. Bake in the preheated oven for 20 minutes or until golden and lovely. Remove from the oven and transfer to a wire rack. Eat fresh fresh fresh.

millet pancakes

Millet is truly one of the world's wonder foods and although it is commonly eaten in China, India and many parts of Africa, it is not so well known in the West. It is full of protein and B vitamins, making it extremely important for vegetarians, and is very 'alkalizing', providing an excellent balance to the acidity of much of the food we eat. Millet is naturally gluten-free and is best used to make flat breads, ie. pancakes, waffles or fritters. Alternatively, it can be used in combination with a gluten flour to make bread.

100 g/¾ cup millet flour

250 ml/1 cup buttermilk, sour milk or 50% plain yogurt and 50% full-fat milk (you can sour milk with lemon juice if you do not have sour milk, yogurt, or buttermilk)

1 egg

1 teaspoon salt

1 tablespoon melted butter, lard or coconut oil

MAKES ENOUGH FOR 6–8 HUNGRY PEOPLE!

Put the flour, buttermilk, sour milk or yogurt-milk, egg and salt in a bowl and whisk with a balloon whisk to combine. Cover and allow to rest for 1 hour, either in or out of the fridge.

Heat up a frying pan and, if necessary, grease it with some of the butter, lard or coconut oil.

Pour the batter into the hot pan – to the size and thickness you like. I like pancakes about 10 cm/4 inches across and rather fat. Others like much larger, much thinner pancakes. It's up to you.

When bubbles form along the edges and on the top, flip the pancake. Make sure to cook the other side properly – 30 seconds to 1 minute.

Remove from the pan and keep warm in a warm oven while you cook the rest of the pancakes.

Eat the pancakes with savoury things like lentils, stew, hummus or curry, or with sweet things like yogurt, honey, maple syrup or jam. Roll them up with a filling like goat cheese and smother them in tomato sauce; or layer them up in a stack with aubergine/eggplant purée in the middle and a simple béchamel sauce on top. There is no end to what you can do with millet pancakes.

Millet has a marvellous, nutty flavour and is a delicious alternative to rice, cous cous or barley when you cook the whole grain and serve it with a meal or in a salad. It also makes great porridge. Friends of mine run a company called Conscious Food and they import millet and millet flour from organic farms in India. They gave me some to play with and I am a true convert. Nobody who eats these millet pancakes will want to go back to normal ones ever again.

Trek though South Africa
An emerging bread culture

The Western Cape was the first place settled by Europeans in what is now the Republic of South Africa. It was established as a Dutch colony in 1652 as a provisioning stop for sailors on their way to the Dutch colonies in the East. At the time, Dutch farmers were offered land so they could grow the food that the sailors needed, and they were the ones who brought wheat there from Europe. Later, the French Huguenots and the English arrived, settling further east into what is now known as the Eastern Cape.

Wars and conflicts caused the mass movement of people of all kinds and ultimately resulted in the 'trek' by the Dutch farmers to the north of the country. They took everything they could carry on their journey, including livestock, furniture and grains, in case they could not find what they needed when they got to where they were going. They also took preserved food such as dried fruit, biltong (dried meat) and rusks

(hard bread) that could be prepared in great quantities in advance and eaten on the go. These are widely eaten today by all communities in South Africa.

When I lived and worked in South Africa in 2002, I travelled widely and ate a great deal, but I never found great bread outside of smart restaurants and guest houses where they baked their own. Stores sold sliced bread in a bag, so if you did not bake or eat out, you did not have much else to choose from. Last year, a friend of mine told me that the bread scene in the Western Cape was booming, so I went on a bread safari to check it out. We were thrilled with the variety and quality, and I was delighted to find so many new, young bakers at bakeries and restaurants throughout the Cape.

Most definitely influenced by the recent influx of Germans who travel to escape the cold winter and cannot live without good bread, even

supermarkets in the Western Cape now sell good sourdough rye bread, and small towns boast great little bakeries where you can talk to the bakers, find out what inspires them, where they buy their flour, and how they learned their craft. Everyone is friendly and generous and I collected recipes from professionals and home cooks alike. There is great quality, simple brown and white bread, bread with local flair such as butternut squash bread, and the more popular European-inspired varieties such as ciabatta, baguette and all sorts of sourdough made from excellent-quality stone-milled rye, wheat and spelt flour.

What interested me even more than this, however, was learning about the two kinds of bread and 'bread kind' that people in South Africa have eaten for years: rusks, which are hard bread; and pap, which is made of maize. Recipes for these abound and I was given some wonderful ones by Libby de Villiers, a chance-met friend who runs Kleinood Farm with her family, and produces award-winning wine and olive oil.

During my bread safari I also learned about steamed bread – also called steamed dumpling bread, imbiza, or amadombolo – the recipe for which I initially saw stitched into a wall hanging in the District Six museum in Cape Town (see photo, left). The lovely ladies at the museum, and later Alicia Giliomee, the talented young chef at Vergelegen wine estate (who called her mum to verify the recipe), explained that in many rural areas and in the squatter camps where people do not have ovens, they have developed a way to steam bread on a Primus stove or over a fire. A basic dough is prepared (you can use the recipe on page 19), proofed, shaped into a ball and put into a plastic bag that is knotted closed, leaving room for the bread to rise. The bag is put on a plate and the whole thing is left in a big pot of steaming water for about an hour. If you have a bread tin, you can put the dough into a tin, then in the plastic bag before steaming in the pot. This method works really well if you can get over your bread being white and slightly sticky rather than golden and crispy, and is certainly a great way to make bread if you don't have an oven.

roti or chapati

Simple to prepare and speedy to make, this dough is best made several hours before the rotis are cooked in order to develop their flavour. If you do not have a lot of time, prepare the dough before you prepare the meal and then fry the rotis at the last minute, serving them one by one or tucking them in a tea towel or napkin to keep them warm. Alternatively, make the dough several hours in advance, cover it and pop it in the fridge. It will keep in the fridge perfectly well for one or two days.

300 g/2⅓ cups wholemeal/whole-wheat flour

200 g/1⅓ cups water

6 g/1½ teaspoons salt

MAKES 20

Put all the ingredients in a bowl and mix them together. Note, there is no yeast in this recipe. Tip out onto the counter and knead well for 10 minutes – see page 12 for instructions on kneading.

Pop the dough back in the bowl and cover it. Allow to rest for as long as you can – see introduction above.

Pull the dough out onto a floured surface.

Divide the dough into 20 equal portions and roll them into balls. cover with a tea towel and allow to rest for 10–15 minutes.

On a floured counter, flatten each ball into a disc and then roll as thinly as possible with a rolling pin.

To fry the rotis, heat a frying pan up. Place a roti in the pan and dry-fry for 10–15 seconds. Flip it over several times, leaving it for 10–15 seconds on each side every time. The roti may or may not puff up in the pan. Remove from the pan and keep warm in wrapped in a tea towel or napkin while you make the rest of the rotis.

If you want a definitely puffy roti, you can buy a long-handled, wire contraption from any Indian store. Transfer a cooked roti to the base of the contraption and then place over the flame of your stove. The roti will puff up just like a football! Be careful when you open it up that you do not burn yourself with the steam.

To eat, tear the rotis into pieces and pick your food up in the pieces with your hands. Indian food will never taste as nice again!

Contrary to popular belief, naan bread is not the staple bread in India. To make naan requires an oven – a tandoor – and few people in India have one of these. Most everyone, however, has access to fire and that is all you need to make roti or chapati, which are two words for the same thing. Made fresh and eaten thrice daily, rotis provide the cosmic balance to Indian meals. Their plain, earthy goodness complements spicy, rich food.

steamed buns

In many parts of the world, people do not cook in ovens. The beautiful and highly varied food in south and east Asia, Africa and parts of the Caribbean, for example, is prepared on the stovetop or over a fire. If people want baked bread, they buy it or they take dough to the communal oven to have it baked for them. Otherwise, they steam it or poach it. Steamed bread has many names and is eaten from Hong Kong to Cape Town to Kingston, Jamaica. Dumplings, amadombolo, imbiza – all of these are different words for steamed bread (see also page 67).

Steamed buns are eaten all over China in many different forms, depending on the region. They are always made with wheat flour; the Chinese consume plenty of wheat flour in the form of bread, cakes and buns. The buns may be sweet – stuffed with a lovely red bean paste, for example; savoury – stuffed with meat and spices, for example; or plain – topped with sesame seeds for decoration. They may be round and hiding a filling, or rolled up and cut up into slices so you can see the filling before biting into it; they may be fluffy or chewy, small or big. But they all have one thing in common: they are steamed. Steaming in a bamboo steamer is best because the flavour of the bamboo is imparted into the bun. However, if you don't have a bamboo steamer, a normal stovetop steamer, electric steamer or rice cooker with a steamer function will work just as well.

300 g/2⅓ cups plain/
all-purpose white wheat flour

1.5 g/¾ teaspoon instant yeast,
3 g/1 teaspoon dry yeast, or
6 g/⅜ cake fresh yeast

200 g/¾ cup water

6 g/1½ teaspoons salt

nigella and sesame seeds,
to decorate

**FOR STUFFED BUNS
(OPTIONAL)**

finely chopped chicken,
pork or tofu

freshly grated ginger

chopped spring onions/
scallions

finely chopped chilli

dark soy sauce

Chinese rice wine

**DIPPING SAUCE
(OPTIONAL)**

equal parts dark soy sauce
and Chinese rice vinegar
mixed with a drop of chilli oil,
if you like

stovetop or electric steamer

MAKES 10

If you are using instant or fresh yeast, put all the ingredients in a big bowl and mix them together. Tip out onto the counter and knead well for 10 minutes – see page 12 for instructions on kneading.

If you are using dry yeast, put the flour in a big bowl and make a well. Sprinkle the dry yeast in the well and add 100 g/½ cup of the water. Cover and allow to rest for 15 minutes. You may or may not get a beige sludge on the top of the water, but don't worry – what is important is to dissolve the yeast. Add the rest of the ingredients and mix. Tip out onto the counter and knead well for 10 minutes – see page 12 for instructions on kneading.

Pop the kneaded dough back into the bowl and cover with a tea towel, shower hat or plastic bag (see page 14). Allow to rest for 1–2 hours until doubled in size.

Cut up 10 squares of wax paper, 5 cm/2 inches by 5 cm/2 inches.

To make plain buns
Pull the dough out onto an unfloured surface and divide it into 10 equal portions. Shape each portion into a tight ball and put each one on a square of wax paper. Lightly flour the tops and cover with a dry tea towel. Allow them rest for 1 hour until doubled in size.

Spray them with water from a plant sprayer and sprinkle sesame or nigella seeds on them. Place them, on their papers, in a steamer full of simmering water and steam for 20 minutes or so. They are done when a knife or a skewer inserted into them comes out clean.

To make stuffed buns
While the dough is rising, stir-fry the chicken, pork or tofu with all the other ingredients and set aside to cool.

When the dough is risen, pull it out onto a floured surface and divide it into 10 equal portions. Roll each portion into a circle no more than ¼ cm/⅛ inch thick. Drain the liquid off the stir-fried ingredients and place a little spoonful in the middle of each circle of dough. [1]

Wet the edges of the circles with water and draw them up into a little parcel, pinching them firmly on the top to close. [2]

Place each parcel on a square of wax paper and dust lightly with flour. Cover them with a tea towel and allow to rest for 1 hour until doubled in size.

Spray them with water from a plant sprayer and sprinkle sesame or nigella seeds on them. [3]

Place them, on their papers, in a steamer full of simmering water and steam for 20 minutes or so. They are done when a knife or a skewer inserted into them comes out clean. [4]

Serve the stuffed or plain buns with the dipping sauce, if you like.

black rice bread

Dutch traders would have taken wheat with them to Indonesia when they first sailed there. Wheat was certainly a Dutch staple and, like any explorers, the Dutch would have taken food and seeds when they set out on their voyages of discovery (see also page 66).

Wheat grows in Southeast Asia but not particularly well, and it is very expensive. It has to be imported from China or Australia. Rice, on the other hand, is the ubiquitous grain. Padding the bread out with rice would have been an inexpensive way of making more bread out of less wheat.

You can use white rice in this wonderful recipe, but black rice is rather more dramatic.

300 g/2⅓ cups strong white (bread) flour

1.5 g/¾ teaspoon instant yeast, 3 g/1 teaspoon dry yeast, or 6 g/⅜ cake fresh yeast

180 g/⅔ cup water

6 g/1½ teaspoons salt (or 1 teaspoon dark soy sauce for an interesting colour and robust flavour)

300 g/2 cups cooked black rice

optional extras: toasted sesame seeds, shredded dried seaweed (like the kind from which sushi rolls are made)

large loaf pan, greased; or small proofing basket, well floured and prepared baking sheet (see page 17)

MAKES 1 LARGE LOAF

If you are using instant or fresh yeast, put all the ingredients (except the rice) in a big bowl and mix them together. Tip out onto the counter and knead well for 10 minutes – see page 12 for instructions on kneading.

If you are using dry yeast, put the flour in a big bowl and make a well. Sprinkle the dry yeast in the well and add 100 g/½ cup of the water. Cover and allow to rest for 15 minutes. You may or may not get a beige sludge on the top of the water, but don't worry – what is important is to dissolve the yeast. Add the rest of the ingredients (except the rice) and mix. Tip out onto the counter and knead well for 10 minutes – see page 12 for instructions on kneading.

Pop the kneaded dough back into the bowl and cover with a tea towel, shower hat or plastic bag (see page 14). Allow to rest for 15 minutes.

Pull the dough out of the bowl and fold in the rice gently. Add any optional extras at this point, too.

Put the dough back in the bowl, cover again and allow to rest for 1–2 hours.

Pull the dough out onto an unfloured surface.

Shaping
Roll the dough into a tight sausage and pop it in the prepared loaf pan or proofing basket. Cover again and allow to rest for 1 hour.

Preheat the oven to 200°C (400°F) Gas 6.

If you have used a pan, pop it in the oven. If you have used a basket, carefully turn the dough out onto the prepared baking sheet.

Bake for 45 minutes. Remove from the oven (and the pan, if using) and transfer to a wire rack.

maritimers' bread

This bread comes from the east coast of Canada and helps you prepare for a long, cold day at sea. It probably originated in Scotland where oats, as the staple crop, would have been added as valuable filler to bread made of relatively more expensive wheat flour. With added butter or lard, and molasses, this is a stick-to-your-ribs kind of bread. You can go fishing all day with a slice or two by your side.

Day One: soaking the oats
Put the oats, raisins, boiling water, salt, molasses and butter, lard or coconut oil in a bowl and mix well. Cover and allow to soak overnight.

Day Two: making the dough
If you are using instant or fresh yeast, put all the ingredients in a big bowl, including the oat mixture, and mix them together. Tip out onto the counter and knead well for 10 minutes – see page 12 for instructions on kneading.

If you are using dry yeast, put the flour in a big bowl and make a well. Sprinkle the dry yeast in the well and add 100 g/½ cup of the water. Cover and allow to rest for 15 minutes. You may or may not get a beige sludge on the top of the water, but don't worry – what is important is to dissolve the yeast. Add the rest of the ingredients, including the oat mixture, and mix. Tip out onto the counter and knead well for 10 minutes – see page 12 for instructions on kneading. The dough will be sticky.

Pop the kneaded dough back into the bowl and cover with a tea towel, shower hat or plastic bag (see page 14). Allow to rest for 1–2 hours until doubled in size.

Pull the dough out onto an unfloured surface.

300 g/2⅓ cups strong white or wholemeal/whole-wheat (bread) flour, or a mixture

1.5 g/¾ teaspoon instant yeast, 3 g/1 teaspoon dry yeast, or 6 g/⅛ cake fresh yeast

150 g/⅔ cup water

FOR THE OATS

½ mug/⅔ cup porridge oats, as unrefined as you can get them, plus extra to sprinkle

big handful of raisins

½ mug/⅔ cup boiling water

4 g/1 teaspoon salt

1 tablespoon molasses/dark treacle

1 tablespoon butter, lard or coconut oil

proofing basket, floured and prepared baking sheet; or loaf pan, greased (see page 17)

MAKES 1 SMALL LOAF

Shaping
Flour your hands to shape the sticky dough into a ball or sausage and put in the prepared proofing basket or baking pan. Cover and allow to rest for 1 hour. Preheat the oven to 200°C (400°F) Gas 6.

If you have used a basket, carefully turn the dough out onto the prepared baking sheet. Sprinkle oats over the top and spray with water to stick them down. Alternatively, sprinkle oats on top of the dough in the pan and spray with water to stick them down. Bake in the preheated oven for 45 minutes. Remove from the oven (and from the pan, if using) and transfer to a wire rack.

anadama bread

There are lots of stories about how this bread got its name. One tells of a fisherman getting angry at his wife Anna for putting cornmeal and molasses into his bread by accident and saying 'Anna, damn it…', which evolved into 'Anadama'. This great bread has been eaten for years by fishermen on the Maritime coast of Canada and northeast coast of the USA to fortify themselves for a hard day at sea.

500 g/4 cups strong white or wholemeal/whole-wheat (bread) flour, or a mixture

2.5 g/1¼ teaspoons instant yeast, 5 g/1¾ teaspoons dry yeast, or 10 g/¾ cake fresh yeast

100 g/scant ½ cup water

FOR THE CORNMEAL

200 g/¾ cup plus 2 tablespoons boiling water

100 g/⅔ cup coarse yellow cornmeal (polenta)

2 tablespoons lard or butter

10 g/2 teaspoons salt

100 g/6 tablespoons molasses/dark treacle or honey

prepared baking sheet (see page 17)

MAKES 2 SMALL LOAVES

As with so many of the different kinds of bread in this book, anadama bread is made using what was cheap and local to pad out the loaf and make it go farther - in this case, ground corn. Whenever you add gluten-free grain or flour to gluten flour, expect a sticky dough and make sure there is plenty of water to help it rise. Dry anadama dough really will bake into bricks.

Day One: soaking the cornmeal

Mix the boiling water, cornmeal, lard, salt and molasses in a big bowl. Cover and allow to soak overnight.

Day Two: making the dough

If you are using instant or fresh yeast, put all the ingredients in a big bowl, including the cornmeal mixture, and mix them together. Tip out onto the counter and knead well for 10 minutes – see page 12 for instructions on kneading.

If you are using dry yeast, put the flour in a big bowl and make a well. Sprinkle the dry yeast in the well and add 100 g/½ cup of the water. Cover and allow to rest for 15 minutes. You may or may not get a beige sludge on the top of the water, but don't worry – what is important is to dissolve the yeast. Add the rest of the ingredients, including the cornmeal mixture, and mix. Tip out onto the counter and knead well for 10 minutes – see page 12 for instructions on kneading. The dough will be sticky.

Pop the kneaded dough back into the bowl and cover with a tea towel, shower hat or plastic bag (see page 14). Allow to rest for 1–2 hours until doubled in size.

Pull the dough out onto a floured surface.

Shaping

Divide the dough into 2. Gently stretch each piece into a rectangle and then fold it up as you would a piece of paper to go into an envelope: fold the bottom edge two-thirds of the way up the rectangle and gently lay it down, then stretch the top edge away from the dough and fold it right over the top of the dough, placing it gently down. Using a scraper, transfer this to the prepared baking sheet. Flour the tops with flour or cornmeal and cover with a dry tea towel. Allow to rest for 45 minutes until doubled in size.

Preheat the oven to 170°C (325°F) Gas 3.

Bake in the preheated oven for 50–60 minutes. Remove from the oven and transfer to a wire rack.

biscuits

Served sweet with butter and honey, savoury with egg, bacon and lard, or simply as a side to mop up gravy, good biscuits are hard to beat. They should be as light as a feather and the trick is to handle the dough as little as possible. If you are a vegetarian, you can use vegetable shortening to make them, but lard makes the very best biscuits. I was given this recipe by my friend Harriet who comes from Tampa, Florida where the biscuits are very good indeed, especially when eaten with some eggs, a side of cheese grits, and a Bloody Mary.

250 g/2 cups plain/all-purpose white wheat flour

2½ teaspoons baking powder

2 g/½ teaspoon salt

80 g/5 tablespoons cold lard or vegetable shortening, cubed, plus extra, melted, to glaze

185 ml/¾ cup buttermilk, sour milk or 50% plain yogurt and 50% full-fat milk (you can sour milk with lemon juice if you do not have sour milk, yogurt, or buttermilk, but if you do, add 1 teaspoon cream of tartar otherwise the bread will not rise very much)

cookie cutter

prepared baking sheet (see page 17)

MAKES LOTS!

Preheat the oven to 230°C (450°F) Gas 8.

Sift together the flour, baking powder and salt in a bowl.

Add the lard and gradually work it in with your fingertips to create small crumbs.

Add the buttermilk, sour milk or yogurt-milk and mix quickly with a fork until the mixture is just blended.

Pull the dough out onto a floured surface and knead lightly just to incorporate all the ingredients.

Shaping

Gently roll out the dough with a rolling pin until 5 cm/2 inches thick. Stamp out rounds with the cookie cutter, dipping the cutter in flour between each cut and making sure not to twist the cutter when you push it in or pull it out. Re-roll the off-cuts of dough and stamp out more rounds. Alternatively, cut the biscuits into squares with a knife.

Place the biscuits on the prepared baking sheet and glaze the tops with melted lard for an even more savoury flavour. For a sweeter flavour, glaze with a mixture of melted butter and honey.

Bake in the preheated oven for 12–15 minutes until golden on the outside and fluffy and soft on the inside. Remove from the oven and transfer to a wire rack.

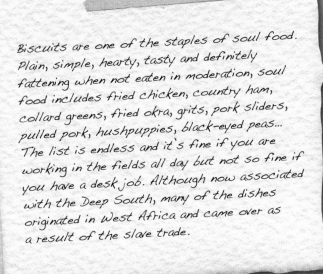

Biscuits are one of the staples of soul food. Plain, simple, hearty, tasty and definitely fattening when not eaten in moderation, soul food includes fried chicken, country ham, collard greens, fried okra, grits, pork sliders, pulled pork, hushpuppies, black-eyed peas... The list is endless and it's fine if you are working in the fields all day but not so fine if you have a desk job. Although now associated with the Deep South, many of the dishes originated in West Africa and came over as a result of the slave trade.

cheese rolls

I first had this bread in Cartegena, Colombia when I was about ten years old. I did not return to Colombia for many years after that but when I finally did, I found it again in Bogotá. It is absolute heaven and so when I was in Toronto a few years ago I made it my business to find a Colombian bakery and beg them for the recipe. The problem is that there are many ways to make these rolls and I have no idea which type I had. I have opted, therefore, for the most simple recipe, made with wheat flour rather than cassava or freshly ground cooked maize, both of which are not always easy to get. Further, because it is not possible to get the soft, stringy Latin American cheese outside of Latin America, the lady in the bakery advised me to use a mixture of cottage cheese and feta cheese.

1 tablespoon butter

200 g/¾ cup plus 1 tablespoon milk

300 g/2⅓ cups plain/all-purpose white wheat flour

1.5 g/¾ teaspoon instant yeast, 3 g/1 teaspoon dry yeast, or 6 g/⅜ cake fresh yeast

3 g/1 scant teaspoon salt

100 g/scant ½ cup cottage cheese or queso fresco

100 g/¾ cup crumbled feta cheese

prepared baking sheet (see page 17)

MAKES 12

Put the butter and milk in a saucepan and heat until the butter has melted and the milk is just about to reach boiling point. Allow to cool to room temperature.

If you are using instant or fresh yeast, put the milk mixture, flour, yeast and salt in a big bowl and mix them together. Tip out onto the counter and knead well for 10 minutes – see page 12 for instructions on kneading.

If you are using dry yeast, put the flour in a big bowl and make a well. Sprinkle the dry yeast in the well and add 100 g/½ cup of the milk mixture. Cover and allow to rest for 15 minutes. You may or may not get a beige sludge on the top of the water, but don't worry – what is important is to dissolve the yeast. Add the remaining milk mixture and the salt and mix. Tip out onto the counter and knead well for 10 minutes – see page 12 for instructions on kneading.

Pop the kneaded dough back into the bowl and cover with a tea towel, shower hat or plastic bag (see page 14). Allow to rest for 10 minutes. Meanwhile, mix up the cheeses into a lumpy blend.

Pull the dough out onto an unfloured surface. Gently fold in the cheeses. You don't want them smeared into the dough – you want the possibility of getting a big mouthful of cheese when you bite into the bread. Put the dough back into the bowl, cover again and allow to rest for 1–2 hours.

Shaping

Pull the dough out onto an unfloured surface and divide it into 12 equal portions. Shape each portion into a loose ball and place 5 cm/2 inches apart on the prepared baking sheet. Cover with a tea towel and allow to rest for 1 hour.

Preheat the oven to 220°C (425°F) Gas 7.

Bake in the preheated oven for 15–20 minutes until golden. To check whether they are done, tap the bottoms of the rolls. If they sound hollow, they are done. If not, pop them back for another 3–4 minutes or so, until they do. Remove from the oven and transfer to a wire rack. Eat any time!

occasional bread

Bread forms the basis of many occasional dishes and is a particular side dish to many occasional meals. Basic bread dough is made just a little bit special when it is turned into pizzas or breadsticks. Thanksgiving dinner is not complete for many families if it is not served with cornbread. You would be as big as a house if you ate brioche every day but on occasion, there is nothing like it. Even the Germans have a guilty secret: fluffy white buns are an adored alternative to the delicious and rather more hearty ryes and sourdoughs that are normally eaten. You can take a little bit more time and bake bread for an occasion – a gorgeous shape, a beautiful topping or a delicious filling make bread special, surprising and even more wonderful.

brioche

Brioche is one of the most famous types of bread in France. Lightly toasted and spread with butter and jam or dipped in egg, it is sublime. There are dozens of ways to make it but the most important fact to accept is this: brioche is all about butter. Remember, as with any enriched dough, brioche has a lot going on that yeast does not like, so making a predough helps achieve a light brioche.

250 g/2 cups plain/all-purpose white wheat flour

1.25 g/½ teaspoon instant yeast, 2.5 g/¾ teaspoon dry yeast, or 5 g/⅜ cake fresh yeast

15 g/1 generous tablespoon sugar

50 g/3½ tablespoons milk, heated up to boiling point, then cooled to room temperature (see page 11)

5 g/1¼ teaspoons salt

2 eggs

125 g/1 stick butter, at room temperature and cubed

melted butter or egg lightly beaten with 1 tablespoon water, to glaze

1 big loaf pan or 2 small loaf pans, greased

MAKES 1 BIG BRIOCHE OR 2 SMALL ONES

Make a predough
Put the flour in a bowl and make a well. Add the yeast and sugar and pour over the milk. Flick some flour on the milk to close the well. Cover and allow to rest for 1 hour. After 1 hour, it will be foamy and bubbling through the top of the well. If it is not, check for signs of life by simply digging through the flour on top of the well.

Making the dough
Sprinkle the salt around the edge of the flour, then add the eggs to the well. Mix and then knead well for 10 minutes – see page 12 for instructions on kneading.

Now add the butter and knead again for 10–20 minutes until the butter is fully incorporated. Don't panic! The dough will get very slack but it will firm up again.

Scrape the dough back into the bowl, cover with a shower hat or plastic bag (see page 14) and allow to rest for 4–6 hours until doubled in size. You can also let it rest in the fridge for 8–12 hours.

If you have left it to rise at room temperature, pop it in the fridge for 1 hour once it has risen because this will make it easier to handle.

Pull the dough out onto an unfloured surface.

Shaping
To make 2 small brioches, divide the dough in half; to make 1 big one, leave it whole. Gently roll the dough into a little sausage and place it in the loaf pan, or bend it into an 'S' by rolling it into a long sausage and folding it, snake-like, into the pan. Or you can divide the dough into 6, roll into balls and tuck them into the pan. Make sure the dough comes only one-third up the pan because it will expand to over twice its original volume. Brush the top with either melted butter or the egg wash, cover again and allow to rest for 30 minutes if the dough is warm, or 2–4 hours if the dough is cold. You want the dough to be warm and well risen before it goes in the oven. Preheat the oven to 180°C (350°F) Gas 4.

Bake in the preheated oven for 30 minutes. Remove from the oven and transfer to a wire rack.

focaccia di Recco

A friend of mine tells me all the time, 'Italy is not one country.' By that he meant that in Italy, as in many places, there are dozens, hundreds and thousands of ways to do anything. Does pizza dough have olive oil in it? Sometimes yes and sometimes no. Does a lasagne have a béchamel sauce? Sometimes yes and sometimes no. Are breadsticks thin or thick, chewy or crispy? Well, it depends on where you live.

This fluidity creates a problem when penning recipes for Italian bread (especially if you are not Italian and therefore have NO legs to stand on). The defence, when you get home and share these recipes with people who then say, 'that's not right', is simply this: Italy is not one country...

Focaccia di Recco is not focaccia as we think we know it (or indeed as most Italians outside of Recco think they know it). It is, however, super easy and absolutely delicious. There is, of course, one more spanner in the works and that is that focaccia di Recco contains 'stracchino' which is a very local cheese. Made from cow's milk, it has a soft texture (not crumbly and not creamy) and a mild flavour. You will have simply to do your best with the soft cheese of your choice!

500 g/4 cups plain/all-purpose or strong white (bread) flour

300 g/1¼ cups water

25 g/2 tablespoons olive oil

10 g/2½ teaspoons salt, plus extra to season

300 g/10 oz. cheese that melts well without being oily (eg. feta, gorgonzola, goat cheese, emmenthal or gruyère, but not cheddar)

olive oil, to drizzle

25-cm/10-inch pie dish/plate, oiled

MAKES 1 BIG FOCACCIA: SERVES 6 AS A MAIN OR 8 AS A STARTER

Put the flour, water, oil and salt in a big bowl and mix them together. Note, there is no yeast in this recipe. Tip out onto the counter and knead well for 15–20 minutes – see page 12 for instructions on kneading. The dough is ready when you can stretch it so thinly that you can see the light through it and there are no lines or markings through the stretched dough.

Pop the dough back in the bowl and cover it. Allow to rest for several hours or overnight at room temperature.

Shaping

Pull the dough out onto an unfloured surface. Divide the dough into 8 equal portions. Cover with a tea towel and allow to rest for 10–15 minutes. Then roll each piece into a tight ball.

On a floured surface, roll one portion with a floured rolling pin into a disc as thin as you can get it. When you cannot roll it any more, pick it up and gently stretch it from the edge, working your way around the circle of dough (use gravity to stretch it) so that you can see light through the whole thing. It should be nearly as thin as paper.

Place the sheet of rolled dough in the pie dish/plate, lining it thoroughly. Make sure the dough spills over the edge of the dish by a good 5–6 cm/2–2½ inches all the way around and that this overhang remains even when you gently push the dough down to line the bottom of the dish. See [picture 1], overleaf.

Do the same thing with 3 more sheets of dough so that you have 4 layers of dough in the dish. See [picture 2], overleaf.

Crumble up or grate the cheese and scatter it on top of the dough in the dish. The cheese should weigh down the sheets of dough

completely on the bottom of the dish. [3]

Now roll the remaining 4 pieces of dough as before and place them, one by one, on top of the cheese in the dish, creating the same overhang as before. [4]

Tear at least 20 little holes in the dough with your fingers or with scissors so that in some places you can see the cheese. The dough should look ragged on the top. [5]

Seal all 8 pieces of dough together by crimping all around the edge of the pie dish. Trim the excess dough with a knife and then, with your fingers, encourage the crimped edges

of the dough away from the top and side of the dish. The dough should not rest on top of the edge of the dish, but inside it.

Preheat the oven to 220°C (425°F) Gas 7.

Drizzle olive oil all over the surface of the dough, then sprinkle some salt on top. Brush it smooth. [6]

Bake the focaccia in the preheated oven for 12–15 minutes or until golden brown. Allow to cool slightly so that the cheese has time to re-set before you serve the focaccia. Eat it warm with a lovely salad. It is perfect for brunch, lunch or a simple dinner.

olive oil bread

This is one of the only rustic breads of Italy that has anything other than salt, water, flour and yeast in it. Olive oil was expensive, so this would have been made for special occasions.

500 g/4 cups plain/all-purpose white wheat flour

2.5 g/1¼ teaspoons instant yeast, 5 g/1¾ teaspoons dry yeast, or 10 g/⅜ cake fresh yeast

250 g/1 cup water

75 g/⅓ cup best olive oil you can afford, plus extra to glaze

10 g/2½ teaspoons salt, plus extra to season

prepared baking sheet (see page 17)

MAKES 12

If you are using instant or fresh yeast, put all the ingredients in a big bowl and mix them together. Tip out onto the counter and knead well for 10 minutes – see page 12 for instructions on kneading.

If you are using dry yeast, put the flour in a big bowl and make a well. Sprinkle the dry yeast in the well and add 100 g/½ cup of the water. Cover and allow to rest for 15 minutes. You may or may not get a beige sludge on the top of the water, but don't worry – what is important is to dissolve the yeast. Add the rest of the ingredients and mix. Tip out onto the counter and knead well for 10 minutes – see page 12 for instructions on kneading.

Pop the kneaded dough back into the bowl and cover with a tea towel, shower hat or plastic bag (see page 14). Allow to rest for 1–2 hours until doubled in size.

Pull the dough out onto an unfloured surface.

Shaping
Divide the dough into 12 equal portions. Shape into tight balls and place in a ring, 1 cm/½ inch apart, on the baking sheet. Cover and rest for 1½ hours.

Preheat the oven to 200°C (400°F) Gas 6. Glaze the buns with olive oil, then sprinkle lightly with salt. Bake in the preheated oven for 30 minutes. Remove from the oven and transfer to a wire rack.

 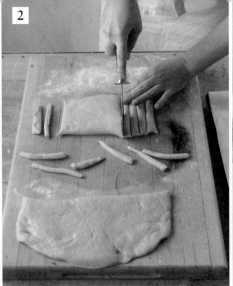 

grissini

Should a breadstick be long, thin and crispy or short, fat and chewy? The answer is: you can have them any way you want. You can make them plain or you can twist them. You can roll them in polenta, sesame seeds or poppy seeds. You can do what you like – they are your grissini!

300 g/⅔ cups plain/all-purpose white wheat flour

1.5 g/¾ teaspoon instant yeast, 3 g/1 teaspoon dry yeast, or 6 g/⅜ cake fresh yeast

200 g/¾ cup plus 1 tablespoon water

6 g/1½ teaspoons salt

1 teaspoon malt syrup (optional – it just adds a bit of colour to the grissini)

1 tablespoon olive oil

optional extras: nigella, sesame and poppy seeds

prepared baking sheet (see page 17)

MAKES 25–30

If you are using instant or fresh yeast, put all the ingredients in a big bowl and mix them together. Tip out onto the counter and knead well for 10 minutes – see page 12 for instructions on kneading.

If you are using dry yeast, put the flour in a big bowl and make a well. Sprinkle the dry yeast in the well and add 100 g/½ cup of the water. Cover and allow to rest for 15 minutes. You may or may not get a beige sludge on the top of the water, but don't worry – what is important is to dissolve the yeast. Add the rest of the ingredients and mix. Tip out onto the counter and knead well for 10 minutes – see page 12 for instructions on kneading.

Shaping
Stretch the dough out on a floured counter into a rectangle about 20 cm/8 inches wide and 1 cm/½ inch thick (and as long as it gets given the other dimensions). Glaze all over with the olive oil, cover with a tea towel or clingfilm/plastic wrap and allow to rest for 1 hour.

Preheat the oven to 220°C (425°F) Gas 7.

Using a pizza cutter or sharp knife, cut the dough into 2 halves, longways. [1]

Cut 'fingers' of dough anywhere from 1–2 cm/½–¾ inch thick. [2]

Stretch each 'finger' as long and as thin as you want, and twist them too if you like. Roll them in the optional extras. [3]

Lay the grissini on the prepared baking sheet. Bake in the preheated oven for 5 minutes for thin ones or 10 minutes for fat ones.

alpine pizza

Up in the Alps where the air is clean and fresh, cows roam and water gurgles on its way down the mountains, there are little huts that provide refreshment to walkers and skiers. Regardless of the country they are in, they serve simple food: pea soup with sausages, sourdough bread with mountain cheeses, simple salads and, if you are lucky, a kind of alpine pizza. These squashy, ovalish flattish pizza-like things are typically made with just about any flour – probably a mixture of wholemeal/whole-wheat or white wheat, or spelt with maybe some rye thrown in for good measure. They are rolled roughly and topped with various simple things like quark (a kind of soft cheese), speck (a kind of bacon) and sliced onions before being popped into a bread oven for a quick little bake. Presented on a plate with no cutlery at all, these are simply crammed into the mouth as soon as possible because they just smell so incredible out in all that air.

300 g/2⅓ cups strong (bread) flour (white, wholemeal/whole-wheat, or a mixture)

1.5 g/¾ teaspoon instant yeast, 3 g/1 teaspoon dry yeast, or 6 g/⅜ cake fresh yeast

180 g/¾ cup water

3 g/¾ teaspoon salt

TOPPINGS (ALL JUST SUGGESTIONS, BUT NO TOMATOES ON ALPINE PIZZAS PLEASE!)

quark cheese (if you cannot get this, mash some cottage cheese and feta into a spreadable paste)

cubed bacon, speck, lardons, pancetta, country ham

thinly sliced onion or shallots

dried mixed herbs

dried mushrooms

and anything you would put on a pizza that you can get in the mountains

semolina or coarse cornmeal, to dust the baking sheet

MAKES 6 SMALL PIZZAS

If you are using instant or fresh yeast, put all the ingredients in a big bowl and mix them together. Tip out onto the counter and knead well for 10 minutes – see page 12 for instructions on kneading.

If you are using dry yeast, put the flour in a big bowl and make a well. Sprinkle the dry yeast in the well and add 100 g/½ cup of the water. Cover and allow to rest for 15 minutes. You may or may not get a beige sludge on the top of the water, but don't worry – what is important is to dissolve the yeast. Add the rest of the ingredients and mix. Tip out onto the counter and knead well for 10 minutes – see page 12 for instructions on kneading.

Pop the kneaded dough back into the bowl and cover with a tea towel, shower hat or plastic bag (see page 14). Allow to rest for 1–2 hours until doubled in size.

Preheat the oven as high as you can get it and put in a baking sheet to heat it up.

Pull the dough out onto a floured surface.

Shaping
Divide the dough into 6 equal portions. One by one, roll them into ovals about ½ cm/¼ inch thick on the floury surface and using a floury rolling pin. Prick each one with a fork several times so it does not puff up in the oven. Spread quark over the pizza bases, leaving a bare border. Top with the toppings of your choice.

Take the VERY HOT baking sheet out of the oven and sprinkle semolina or coarse cornmeal over it. Using a scraper or spatula, carefully transfer the pizzas to the sheet and pop them in the oven for 10 minutes or so until they are clearly cooked (tops bubbling, dough browned). This depends on how hot you can get your oven. Remove from the oven and transfer to a wire rack. Eat hot, but don't burn yourself by eating them too quickly!

semmel rolls

Germany is justifiably famous for its bread. Spelt bread, rye bread, bread with seeds, bread with nuts – it's all absolutely fantastic. There is one wonderful weakness that the Germans have regarding bread: fluffy white rolls. You find them on the breakfast table, in hotels and guest houses, at markets where you can buy a sausage and receive a fluffy white roll. What is special about them is their fluffy texture. What is lovely about them is their beauty. The tops are slashed in a pattern that identifies them as fluffy white rolls!

1 kg/8 cups strong white (bread) flour

600 g/2½ cups water

5 g/2½ teaspoons instant yeast, 10 g/3¾ teaspoons dry yeast, or 20 g/1¼ cakes fresh yeast

20 g/1½ tablespoons salt

seeds, to decorate (optional)

prepared baking sheets (see page 17)

MAKES ABOUT 30

Day One: making a predough
Put in a bowl: 250 g/2 cups of the flour, 300 g/1¼ cups of the water and the yeast. Mix, then cover with a dry tea towel and allow to rest overnight.

Day Two: making the dough
Add the remaining flour, water and the salt to the predough and mix. Tip out onto the counter and knead well for 10 minutes – see page 12 for instructions on kneading.

Pop the kneaded dough back in the bowl and cover with a tea towel, shower hat or plastic bag (see page 14). Allow to rest for 2 hours.

Pull the dough out onto an unfloured surface.

Shaping
Shape the dough into a tight sausage and divide it into about 30 portions, depending on how big you want the rolls. Cover with a tea towel and allow to rest for 15 minutes.

Form the portions of dough into tight balls. Place them 5 cm/ 2 inches apart on the prepared baking sheets. Cover with a tea towel and allow to rest for 1 hour.

Preheat the oven to 220°C (425°F) Gas 7.

Make slashes in the tops of the rolls with a sharp knife or scissors – this could be a flower pattern, a swirly pattern, or just a simple cut from one side to the other.

Spray the rolls with fresh water from a plant sprayer and, if you would like to, decorate them with seeds.

Bake the rolls in the preheated oven for 15–20 minutes until golden. To check whether they are done, tap the bottoms of the rolls. If they sound hollow, they are done. If not, pop them back for another 3–4 minutes or so, until they do. Remove from the oven and transfer to a wire rack.

You can divide this recipe in half if you want to.

beer bread

Which came first – beer or bread? I have no idea, but I do know that beer has long been used all over the world to bake bread. Although now more expensive than water, we do need to remember that beer was drunk (and in some countries is still drunk) in many cases because it was more widely available than drinking water. As the internal temperature of bread is only 98°C/208°F, bread is not sterile and so dirty water used in bread will make you as sick as if you drank the water. If you are not sure (and let's face it – even if you are) use beer instead of water! It makes a great-tasting loaf.

250 g/2 cups wholemeal/
whole-wheat flour

50 g/⅓ cup dark or light
rye flour

1.5 g/¾ teaspoon instant yeast,
3 g/1 teaspoon dry yeast, or
6 g/⅜ cake fresh yeast

220 g/7½ oz. beer, at room
temperature

6 g/1½ teaspoons salt

*small proofing basket, well
floured, and a prepared baking
sheet; or a loaf pan, greased
(see page 17)*

MAKES 1 SMALL LOAF

If you are using instant or fresh yeast, put all the ingredients in a big bowl and mix them together. Tip out onto the counter and knead well for 10 minutes – see page 12 for instructions on kneading.

If you are using dry yeast, put the flours in a big bowl and make a well. Sprinkle the dry yeast in the well and add 100 g/½ cup of the beer. Cover and allow to rest for 15 minutes. You may or may not get a beige sludge on the top of the water, but don't worry – what is important is to dissolve the yeast. Add the rest of the ingredients and mix. Tip out onto the counter and knead well for 10 minutes – see page 12 for instructions on kneading. The dough will be sticky. Pause to appreciate the beery aroma as you knead!

Pop the kneaded dough back into the bowl and cover with a tea towel, shower hat or plastic bag (see page 14). Allow to rest for 1–2 hours until doubled in size.

Pull the dough out onto an unfloured surface.

Shaping

Flour your hands, shape the dough into a ball or sausage and pop it in the prepared proofing basket or loaf pan. Cover again and allow to rest for 1 hour until doubled in size.

Preheat the oven to 200°C (400°F) Gas 6.

If proofing in a basket, carefully turn the dough out onto the prepared baking sheet and pop in the oven. If baking in a pan, pop the pan in the oven. Bake for about 45 minutes. To check whether it is done, tap the bottom of the loaf. If it sounds hollow, it is done. If not, pop it back for another 5 minutes or so, until it does. Remove from the oven and transfer to a wire rack.

Brewer's yeast and baker's yeast are different, although it would take a microbiologist to explain exactly how. Although there are ancient pictures of monks skimming the foamy top out of the beer vat and putting it into bread dough, it is unlikely that the yeast in the beer on its own was the only thing helping the bread to rise. You can try this beer bread without yeast if you like, but you may get a rather worthy loaf. Send pictures if you do!

scalded rye bread

My Swedish friends introduced me to this incredible bread on a picnic and it had a soft, soft crumb, almost the texture of a cake. I found out that what made it soft was not added fat but 'scalded flour'. Trust me and try this. You need to start the night before, be comfortable with sticky dough and bake it at a lower temperature.

650 g/5¼ cups strong white (bread) flour (you can use wholemeal/whole-wheat, but I find you taste the scalded flour better with white – try both and let me know what you think)

4 g/2 teaspoons instant yeast, 8 g/2¾ teaspoons dry yeast, or 16 g/1 cake fresh yeast

250 g/1 cup water

15 g/1½ tablespoons salt

FOR SCALDING THE RYE FLOUR

100 g/¾ cup dark rye flour

300 g/1¼ cups boiling water

prepared baking sheet (see page 17)

MAKES 2 SMALL LOAVES

Day One: scalding the rye flour
Put the rye flour and boiling water in a bowl and mix into a stiff paste. Cover and allow to soak overnight.

Day Two: making the dough
If you are using instant or fresh yeast, put all the ingredients in a big bowl, including the rye mixture, and mix them together. Tip out onto the counter and knead well for 10 minutes – see page 12 for instructions on kneading.

If you are using dry yeast, put the flour in a big bowl and make a well. Sprinkle the dry yeast in the well and add 100 g/½ cup of the water. Cover and allow to rest for 15 minutes. You may or may not get a beige sludge on the top of the water, but don't worry – what is important is to dissolve the yeast. Add the rest of the ingredients, including the rye mixture, and mix. Tip out onto the counter and knead well for 10 minutes – see page 12 for instructions on kneading. The dough will be sticky.

Pop the kneaded dough back into the bowl and cover with a tea towel, shower hat or plastic bag (see page 14). Allow to rest for 2 hours.

Pull the dough out onto a floured surface.

Shaping
Divide the dough into 2. Flour your hands and gently stretch each piece into a rectangle 2 cm/¾ inch thick and then fold it up as you would a piece of paper to go into an envelope: fold the bottom edge two-thirds of the way up the rectangle and gently lay it down, then stretch the top edge away from the dough and fold it right over the top of the dough, placing it gently down. Using a scraper, transfer this to a floured tea towel. Cover with another floured tea towel and allow to rest for 1 hour.

Preheat the oven to 230°C (450°F) Gas 8.

Move the loaves to the prepared baking sheet, pop in the oven and immediately lower the temperature to 180°C (350°F) Gas 4. Bake for 40 minutes. Remove from the oven and transfer to a wire rack.

blinis

Buckwheat is grown all over Russia and central Asia. Nutritious and delicious, it is eaten as porridge (kasha) or milled into flour and made into a variety of things including blinis – little pancakes. As buckwheat has no gluten, you can never expect it to make a risen bread but it does make fabulous pancakes.

They puff up a bit in the pan due to the fermentation that is caused by soaking the flour in an acidic dairy product (in Russia they use something called Smetana but if you cannot get it, you can use sour cream, sour milk, buttermilk or half-yogurt-half-milk). Blinis have quite a strong flavour which carry smoked fish and, of course, caviar, very well indeed. If you cannot afford caviar, butter them when they are warm and load them up with finely chopped onion, capers, and hard-boiled eggs. Vodka strictly optional.

200 g/1½ cups buckwheat flour

50 g/½ cup plain/all-purpose white wheat flour

pinch of instant yeast, ½ teaspoon dry yeast, or 1 g/⅛ cake fresh yeast

100 ml/scant ½ cup milk, heated up to boiling point, then cooled to room temperature (see page 11)

1 egg, separated

400 ml/1⅔ cups sour cream, buttermilk, sour milk (full-fat is best), 50% plain yogurt and 50% full-fat milk, crème fraîche or keffir – any sour milk product will do

4 g/1 teaspoon salt

2 tablespoons butter, melted and slightly cooled, plus extra for frying

MAKES LOTS!

Making a predough

Sift the flours into a bowl and make a well. Add the yeast and pour over the milk. Flick some flour on the milk to close the well. Cover and allow to rest for 30 minutes. After 30 minutes, it will be foamy and bubbling through the top of the well. If it is not, check for signs of life by simply digging through the flour on top of the well.

Making the dough

Add the egg yolk, sour cream, salt and melted butter to the predough and stir well with a balloon whisk to get out all the bumps and lumps. (Reserve the egg white until you are ready to make the blinis.) Cover and allow to rest for 1 hour (or several hours in the fridge).

Just before you are ready to make the blinis, beat the egg white into soft peaks form and fold it into the batter.

Heat up a frying pan and add some butter. When it is sizzling, ladle in the batter to make little pancakes about 4–6 cm/1¾–2¼ inches in diameter, depending on how large you would like them. When bubbles form on top of the blinis and the edges go brown, flip them over. Make sure you cook them on the flipped side too! There is nothing as lame as an uncooked blini.

If you are serving them straightaway, stack them up on a plate and keep them warm until they are all cooked. You can cook these in advance and keep them well wrapped in the fridge or in an airtight container for a couple of days. They also freeze very well. To liven them up, simply warm them up in the oven.

Variation: You can use just buckwheat flour if you would like to or need to because of a gluten allergy or intolerance. If you do, the blinis will be a little more fragile. So, flip them really carefully and be mindful of the fact that they will break quite easily.

Discover Armenia
The cradle of bread

'We Armenians are made of 50% bread and 50% soup.'

My bread journey in Armenia included visiting Hatsavan ('Hats' means bread and 'Avan' means village) where we chanced on a family baking bread. In one day, the ladies use 50 kg/110 lbs flour to make 94 kg/207 lbs bread – enough to last for a month. Apples, coffee, nuts, sweets, homemade cheese, warm bread, homemade wine and vodka were offered to us in the sunny orchard outside the bake house. I also met a wonderful family headed up by Fatima and her husband Gagik, who live in the village of Sarnakhbiur. They postponed their baking by a day in order to wait for us when we were delayed by the snow. I was welcomed like family, fed every possible delicacy until I nearly burst, and was taught to

make and shape both 'lavage' and 'bocon', two types of bread baked on the side of the clay oven fired by wood, and built into the floor of the bake house. I also visited a gorgeous restaurant called Cherkezi Dzor in Gyumri where the cooks taught me how to make 'gata', a cake baked in a tin, on a trivet, in a wood-fired bread oven. Bread is a serious business in Armenia and the people were delighted to show me how it is done.

In the National Museum in the capital, Yerevan, there is a sickle that dates back to the sixth millennium BCE. It comes from the western Armenian Highlands – now in eastern Turkey – and proves categorically that people living there were harvesting crops 8,000 years ago. Where they were harvesting crops they were definitely settled: keeping livestock, making food and

baking bread. In the Armenian mountains there are places protected by the government where original wheat still grows wild. Bread, the Armenians argue, was born in Armenia. When I asked the director of the National Museum, Anelka Grigorian, what bread meant to Armenians, she sat back and looked at me, overwhelmed. Silent for a few moments, she then put her fingers over her eyes. 'Bread,' she concluded, 'is so meaningful to us that I cannot articulate it right now. I will have to think about this deeply and then write to you.'

Bread is connected to all things in Armenia but what is common throughout is that bread is sacred: there is a worship of bread in every family and they have not lost this. The oven was the altar in villages where there was no church – people were married and children were baptized there. In the same way that Armenians back out of a church so as not to turn their backs on the altar, many people still leave their houses in the same way to avoid turning their backs on the hearth, the place where bread is baked and life is celebrated.

There is a correct way to hold bread and a correct way to place it on the table – in the centre. There are daily rituals regarding bread that are partly connected to Christianity (Armenia was the first Christian country) and more strongly connected to life as it has been lived through the ages. Nobody (and it's true) allows bread to stay on the floor or the ground. If bread drops, it is immediately picked up and either eaten (if you are at home), disposed of properly (if you are not at home), or even placed on a high window sill (if you are on the street) – elevating it off the ground as befits its status in society.

The word for bread is the same as the word for food, home, family and life itself. 'Have you had bread' means 'have you eaten' and to be 'without bread' can mean that you are without a home, without a family, and indeed without a life. A person can be described as a 'bread person' if they are particularly generous and respected; and a home can be described as a 'bread home' if it is gracious and generous.

lahmajo

Lahmajo is to Armenians what pizza is to Italians. The difference is that lahmajo is only ever topped with cheese and that you would never use a knife and fork to eat it. Frequently shared (because who would ever want to eat alone?) lahmajo is always eaten by hand and served with butter for extra deliciousness!

Now you can get lahmajo in little kiosks by the side of the road and you frequently see people carrying flat boxes of it back home or to their offices. It is rare to see people eating it on the street, maybe because eating on the street is bad manners, or because you cannot really share it like this. Most likely it is because you risk dropping some of it if you eat it on the go. In Armenia, if you drop bread by accident, you always (and I mean always) pick it up and place it somewhere higher (a window ledge, a tree) or dispose of it properly. Bread is sacred. Find out more on pages 106–107.

400 g/3 cups strong white (bread) flour

2 g/1 teaspoon instant yeast, 4 g/1¼ teaspoons dry yeast, or 8 g/½ cake fresh yeast

270 ml/1 cup plus 1 tablespoon water

50 g/3 tablespoons butter

6 g/1½ teaspoons salt

TOPPING

plenty of strong cheese, grated or crumbled, eg. cheddar or feta

coarsely ground black pepper

poppy seeds

dried mixed herbs

paprika, if you like it

4 baking sheets, oiled

MAKE 4 BIG LAHMAJOS

If you are using instant or fresh yeast, put all the ingredients in a big bowl and mix them together. Tip out onto the counter and knead well for 10 minutes – see page 12 for instructions on kneading.

If you are using dry yeast, put the flour in a big bowl and make a well. Sprinkle the dry yeast in the well and add 100 g/½ cup of the water. Cover and allow to rest for 15 minutes. You may or may not get a beige sludge on the top of the water, but don't worry – what is important is to dissolve the yeast. Add the rest of the ingredients and mix. Tip out onto the counter and knead well for 10 minutes – see page 12 for instructions on kneading.

Pop the kneaded dough back into the bowl and cover with a tea towel, shower hat or plastic bag (see page 14). Allow to rest for 1–2 hours until doubled in size.

Pull the dough out onto a floured surface.

Shaping
Divide the dough into 4 equal portions and shape into loose balls. Cover with a tea towel and allow to rest for 15 minutes.

Preheat the oven to 230°C (450°F) Gas 8.

On a well floured surface, roll a portion of dough into a rectangle about 25 x 35 cm/10 x 14 inches and place on a prepared baking sheet. Prick with a fork several times so it does not puff up in the oven. Sprinkle lots of cheese over the base, leaving a bare border. Sprinkle pepper, poppy seeds, dried herbs and paprika on top of the cheese. Bake in the preheated oven for 15 minutes or until golden brown and bubbling.

Just before it is done, prepare the next one, then pop it in the oven to bake while you let the first one cool slightly and eat it. Remember – this is a group activity! Share each lahmajo and eat them one by one while the other ones cook. Serve with extra butter, if you like!

khachapuri

As a teen, I was invited to the then USSR (I am dating myself horribly now) and travelled around for three weeks and loved it. I specifically loved Tbilisi, Samarkand and Leningrad both for the atmosphere, the people, the markets and the bread. In Tbilisi, we exchanged high school T-shirts and Adidas-branded clothing for jars and jars of the best caviar (which we ate off pen knives for lack of anything else), chocolate and vodka. In Samarkand we remarked at the beauty of the ruined mosques and in Leningrad we ate ice cream and drank Champagne at an amazingly baroque and thoroughly non-communist café on Nevsky Prospekt. In general, the food was rather bland, stodgy and heavy. However, I remember the bread with great enthusiasm.

Khachapuri is from Georgia and is filled with all sorts of things. Typically it is filled with cheese, but you can find it filled with meat or eggs too. Adjarian, Imeretian, Abkhazian and Ossetian are but four of the many kinds you can find if you travel in that lovely region of the world.

500 g/4 cups strong white (bread) flour

2.5 g/1¼ teaspoons instant yeast, 5 g/1½ teaspoons dry yeast, or 10 g/⅜ cake fresh yeast

250 g/1 cup water

50 g/3 tablespoons butter, plus extra, melted, to glaze

½ teaspoon ground coriander

10 g/2½ teaspoons salt

FILLING

2 eggs

250 g/8 oz. cooked diced potato, cooked minced/ground meat, or non-oily cheese (eg. mixture of feta and cottage cheese, or goat cheese and mozzarella)

2 tablespoons strong white (bread) flour

2 g/½ teaspoon salt

1 teaspoon paprika

prepared baking sheet (see page 17)

MAKES 1 BIG LOAF

For the filling, mix together all the ingredients, cover and set aside until you need them.

If you are using instant or fresh yeast, put all the ingredients in a big bowl and mix them together. Tip out onto the counter and knead well for 10 minutes – see page 12 for instructions on kneading.

If you are using dry yeast, put the flour in a big bowl and make a well. Sprinkle the dry yeast in the well and add 100 g/½ cup of the water. Cover and allow to rest for 15 minutes. You may or may not get a beige sludge on

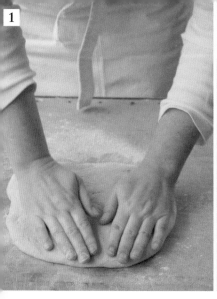

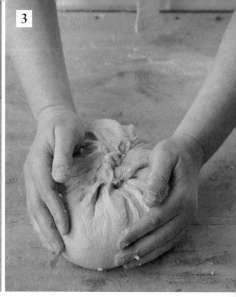

the top of the water, but don't worry – what is important is to dissolve the yeast. Add the rest of the ingredients and mix. Tip out onto the counter and knead well for 10 minutes – see page 12 for instructions on kneading.

Pop the kneaded dough back into the bowl and cover with a tea towel, shower hat or plastic bag (see page 14). Allow to rest for 1–2 hours until doubled in size.

Pull the dough out onto a floured surface.

Shaping

As ever, there is not one shape for khachapuri, but several. The idea is to stuff the dough with the filling and you can make one big one or lots of little ones. I like to make one big one and cut it into slices or wedges.

Roll the dough into a big circle (or several small circles) 1 cm/½ inch thick. [1]

Spoon some filling into the middle of the dough and then wet the edges of the dough with some water.

Take one edge of the dough pull it toward the middle. Pick up another edge of dough and pull it up, making a pleat, and sticking it to the first piece of dough. [2]

Pleat the rest of the dough in this fashion to cover the filling completely and then twist the dough in the middle to make a knot. [3]

Transfer the parcel of dough to the prepared baking sheet. Glaze the dough with melted butter. Make 4 evenly spaced slits in the dough that start at the top (where the dough is bunched) and go about halfway down the side of the parcel.

Cover with a tea towel and allow to rest for 1 hour.

Preheat the oven to 200°C (400°F) Gas 6.

Pop it in the preheated oven and bake for 45 minutes until golden brown. Remove from the oven and transfer to a wire rack.

chickpea pudding

Gram flour is used a great deal in Indian cooking. It is perfect for vegetarians as it is simply ground up chickpeas and so is packed full of protein. This dish is very savoury, delicious and filling – a little goes a long way. Serve with plain rice and yogurt or jazz up the rice and yogurt with spices and/or vegetables for a simple, elegant Indian meal. The alternative is to go multi-cultural and serve it with a simple salad and a glass of dry white wine.

200 g/1½ cups chickpea flour
(also known as gram flour)

½ teaspoon ground turmeric

½ teaspoon garam masala

4 g/1 teaspoon salt

200 g/¾ cup plus 1 tablespoon
plain yogurt

400 g/1⅔ cups water

½ teaspoon fennel seeds

½ teaspoon cumin seeds

pinch of ground asafoetida

*23-cm/9-inch pie dish/plate,
well greased*

SERVES 8

Put the flour, turmeric, garam masala and salt in a bowl and blend well with your hands. Add the yogurt and the water and whisk with a balloon whisk to combine. It will be lumpy but don't worry about that just yet.

Dry fry the fennel and cumin seeds in a pan until they smell fragrant, then add the asafoetida. Scrape into the bowl of batter and blend again. Cover and allow to rest for 1 hour (or overnight in the fridge) until the flour is all absorbed and the lumps are gone.

Preheat the oven to 220°C (425°F) Gas 7.

Whisk up the batter and pour it in the prepared pie dish/plate. Bake in the preheated oven for 30–40 minutes or until golden and thoroughly set.

Allow to cool slightly while you make rice or salad (or rice salad!) and side dishes. Serve just warm.

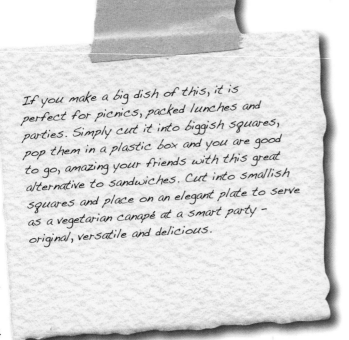

If you make a big dish of this, it is perfect for picnics, packed lunches and parties. Simply cut it into biggish squares, pop them in a plastic box and you are good to go, amazing your friends with this great alternative to sandwiches. Cut into smallish squares and place on an elegant plate to serve as a vegetarian canapé at a smart party – original, versatile and delicious.

bridge rolls

It is unclear where the name 'bridge rolls' comes from. Some say it is because they look like bridges but I have always associated them with bridge parties – I have seen plenty of movies and television shows from the 50s and 60s when ladies who played bridge ate sandwiches on tiny little rolls. When I first tried one, I was delighted at their buttery flavour and delicate texture. The key is to make them tiny – 50 g/1¾ oz. at most – so they look beautifully delicate. You too can pretend you are a lady who lunches!

450 g/3⅔ cups plain/all-purpose white wheat flour

2.25 g/1⅛ teaspoons instant yeast, 4.5 g/1½ teaspoons dry yeast, or 9 g/⅔ cake fresh yeast

200 g/¾ cup plus 1 tablespoon milk that you have warmed to boiling point and then let cool right down (if you are feeling really decadent you can use cream)

9 g/2¼ teaspoons salt

2 eggs

100 g/6½ tablespoons butter, at room temperature and cubed

1 egg lightly beaten with 1–2 tablespoons milk, to glaze

prepared baking sheet (see page 17)

MAKES ABOUT 25

Making a predough

Put the flour in a bowl and make a well. Add the yeast and pour over the milk. Flick some flour on the milk to close the well. Cover and allow to rest for 1 hour. After 1 hour, it will be foamy and bubbling through the top of the well. If it is not, check for signs of life by simply digging through the flour on top of the well.

Making the dough

Sprinkle the salt around the edge of the flour, then add the eggs to the well. Mix and then knead well for 10 minutes – see page 12 for instructions on kneading. It will be rather dry and not easy to knead but you just have to persevere.

Now add the butter and knead again for 10 minutes until the butter is fully incorporated.

Scrape the dough back into the bowl, cover with a tea towel, shower hat or plastic bag (see page 14) and allow to rest until doubled in size – 12 hours in the fridge or 6 hours at room temperature.

Pull the dough out onto an unfloured surface.

Shaping

Divide the dough into 25 portions, each weighing no more than 50 g/1¾ oz. Cover with a dry tea towel and allow to rest for 5 minutes. Shape each portion into a tight ball and roll into tight sausages. Pick up one sausage and move it away from you. Roll it toward you as follows:

i) start with your hands together in the middle of each sausage, thumbs completely touching;

ii) roll toward you as you move your wrists – not your hands – apart – so that the fingertips of the index finger of each hand meet and then the fingertips of the middle finger of each hand meet. As you do that, the palms of your hands travel effortlessly over the surface of the dough, stretching it out without applying any downward pressure.

iii) pick up the dough, move it away from you and roll again as above. Do this as many times as you need to get a bridge roll 10 cm/4 inches long and 2 cm/¾ inch in diameter.

Place the bridge rolls on the prepared baking sheet, either 2 cm/¾ inch apart or closer together – whatever you have room for. Cover with a dry tea towel and allow to rest until doubled in size – 2 hours if the dough is warm, or 4 hours if the dough is cold.

Preheat the oven to 200°C (400°F) Gas 6.

Glaze the tops with the egg wash, pop in the preheated oven and immediately lower the temperature to 180°C (350°F) Gas 4. Bake for 15 minutes until pale gold and they sound hollow when tapped. Remove from the oven and transfer to a wire rack.

cornbread

Although typically eaten as a savoury accompaniment to a meal, you can pour maple syrup or put maple sugar on top of cornbread to turn make it sweet. Alternatively, you can add sugar or honey to the mixture to turn it into a bit of a cake.

Although no longer a staple bread, many north Americans eat cornbread in one of its many forms, regularly.This recipe for cornbread is not sweet and although it calls for the bread to be baked, it is traditionally cooked on the stovetop or over a fire.

Maize is one of indigenous grains in the Americas. Indigenous people ground corn and mixed it with milk or water and fat into a thick batter which was then cooked over a fire. The addition of butter, baking powder, bicarbonate of soda/baking soda, salt and eggs makes it a little richer and more familiar than the original would have been.

300 g/2¼ cups coarse cornmeal

480 ml/2 cups full-fat sour milk, buttermilk or 50% plain yogurt and 50% full-fat milk (you can sour milk with lemon juice if you do not have sour milk, yogurt, or buttermilk, but if you do, add 1 teaspoon cream of tartar otherwise the bread will not rise very much)

180 g/¾ cup animal fat, eg. lard, dripping, bacon fat, goose fat or a combination (butter will burn)

1 teaspoon baking powder

1 teaspoon bicarbonate of soda/baking soda

3 g/¾ teaspoon salt

2 eggs

ovenproof, flameproof frying pan or dish, at least 25 cm/ 10 inches in diameter

SERVES 10–12

Preheat the oven to 220°C (425°F) Gas 7 and move an oven shelf up to the upper-middle position. You will need to get your frying pan in there as high as possible.

Put the cornmeal in the frying pan over medium heat and dry fry, stirring constantly until you begin to smell it. Be careful not to burn it.

Pour the roasted cornmeal into a large bowl, add the sour milk and mix well. Set aside.

Put the frying pan back over the heat, add the fat and heat until it is smoking.

Turn off the burner and pour all except about 2 tablespoons of the melted fat into the bowl with the cornmeal. Retain the remaining fat in the pan. Add the rest of the ingredients to the cornmeal mixture in the bowl and whisk with a balloon whisk to combine.

Pour the mixture back into the pan and bake on the upper-middle shelf of the preheated oven for 12–15 minutes until the top is golden and cracked and it has come away from the sides.

Remove from the oven and allow to cool in the pan for 5 minutes, then turn out onto a wire rack to cool before slicing.

This is stupendously good with a cooked breakfast (pancakes and syrup optional extras outside of North America), with a hearty soup, or to soak up gravy with a gamey stew or sauce.

Variation: To fry rather than bake the cornbread, instead of putting the pan in the oven, put it over low heat on the stove and cook the bread slowly. Spend 3 minutes with the flame under the middle of the pan and then 3 minutes each with the flame under the top, bottom, right, and left of the pan. Entertain yourself by flipping the cornbread over – use a plate that is slightly smaller than the pan, invert the bread onto the plate and then slide it back into the pan and cook for another 3 minutes. It's easier in the oven…!

celebration bread

Bread is used in celebrations all over the world. Enriching it with expensive ingredients like eggs, fats, milk, spices, dried fruit, nuts, seeds, olives, cheese and meat honours guests as well as occasions. From India to Romania to Argentina, there are many different kinds of celebration bread. Some have rich dough and are beautifully shaped, others are made of plain dough and are stuffed with gorgeous ingredients to turn any occasion into a celebration.

Sadly, it is possible to get many of the different kinds of celebration bread in supermarkets all year round. While this may be convenient, it does rob the bread of its significance, and takes away our opportunity to dream about it when we cannot get it. You can give your friends and family back the opportunity to dream by making celebration bread at home in its season! Although the ingredients are no longer considered to be luxurious, celebration bread is a bit fiddly to put together and this means the homemade versions taste superior in every way and makes them extra special. The expressions on the faces of friends and family when you present them with your celebration bread will give you all the affirmation and confidence you need to continue baking it at home.

hot cross buns

Hot cross buns should be light, spicy and fruity. Traditionally available in the UK only on Good Friday, the cross symbolizes the crucifixion of Christ. Today you can get them almost every day of the year from a supermarket but even the spices and sugar cannot disguise the taste of the preservatives and the additives. There is just no substitute for a homemade bun, hot out of the oven, toasted or made into the most amazing bread and butter pudding.

Put the sultanas/raisins in a little bowl and just cover them with water. Give them a little stir every once in a while.

Making a predough
Put the flours in a big bowl, mix them by hand and make a well. Add the yeast and sugar to the well and pour in the milk. Flick some flour on the milk to close the well. Cover and allow to rest for 1 hour. After 1 hour, it will be foamy and bubbling through the top of the well. If it is not, check for signs of life by simply digging through the flour on top of the well.

Making the dough
Sprinkle the salt around the edge of the flour, then add the butter, egg and spices to the well. Mix and then knead well for 10 minutes – see page 12 for instructions on kneading. Pop it back in the bowl, cover with a tea towel and allow to rest for 15 minutes.

Drain the raisins and gently knead into the dough. Pop the dough back in the bowl, cover with a tea towel, shower hat or plastic bag (see page 14) and allow to rest for 2 hours until doubled in size.

Pull the dough out onto an unfloured surface.

Shaping
Divide the dough into 15 equal portions. Shape into tight balls between lightly floured hands. Place about 5 cm/2 inches apart on the prepared roasting dishes. Cover with a tea towel and allow to rise for 45 minutes.

Preheat the oven to 200°C (400°F) Gas 6.

For the crosses, whisk all the ingredients together in a bowl. Spoon into a piping bag or a little plastic bag and cut a tiny hole in the corner. Squeeze the bag gently to get all the mixture gathered near the hole and then carefully pipe crosses on each risen bun.

Bake in the preheated oven for 18–20 minutes until (hopefully) the bun is golden brown but the cross is still white. Remove from the oven and transfer to a wire rack. Glaze the buns immediately with liquid honey, golden syrup, corn syrup or the glaze of your choice.

250 g/1⅔ cups sultanas/raisins

150 g/1 cup wholemeal/whole-wheat flour

300 g/2⅓ cups plain/all-purpose white wheat flour

2 g/1 teaspoon instant yeast, 4.5 g/1½ teaspoons dry yeast, or 9 g/⅝ cake fresh yeast

50 g/¼ cup sugar

280 g/1¼ cups milk, heated up to boiling point, then cooled to room temperature (see page 11)

9 g/2¼ teaspoons salt

50 g/3 tablespoons butter

1 egg

5 teaspoons ground spices, eg. 2 teaspoons cinnamon, 1 teaspoon mixed/apple pie spice, 1 teaspoon ginger, ½ teaspoon cloves, ½ teaspoon allspice

FOR THE CROSSES

50 g/⅓ cup plain/all-purpose white wheat flour

pinch of baking powder

½ teaspoon vegetable oil

50 g/3 tablespoons cold water

deep roasting dishes, lined with parchment paper

MAKES 15

stollen

Stollen is a traditional German Christmas cake that originates in Dresden. It is made with an enriched dough full of dried fruit and almonds that have been soaked in high-proof rum or brandy to preserve the cake while it matures. Some stollen has a sausage of marzipan baked into the middle which is supposed to symbolize the baby Jesus wrapped in His swaddling clothes. That is not the kind I grew up with, so I don't like it, but there is no reason why you cannot do it if you like the sound of it.

I had never been happy with the recipes I tried and so I turned to my German friend, Jules. She asked her friend Simone who kindly volunteered this excellent recipe. You can substitute butter for the lard if you must and add a sausage of marzipan if you want it, but above all please store this for at least six weeks before you eat it. Well wrapped, it will keep for three to four months.

250 g/2 cups plain/all-purpose white wheat flour

1 g/¾ teaspoon instant yeast, 2.5 g/1 teaspoon dry yeast, or 5 g/⅜ cake fresh yeast

35 g/3 tablespoons sugar

65 g/¼ cup milk, heated up to boiling point, then cooled to room temperature (see page 11)

5 g/1¼ teaspoons salt

25 g/2 tablespoons lard

grated zest of ½ lemon

65 g/4 tablespoons butter, at room temperature and cubed

SOAKING THE FRUIT AND NUTS

200 g/1⅓ cups raisins

60 g/½ cup flaked/slivered almonds

25 g/3 tablespoons mixed candied peel

60 g/¼ cup rum or brandy (the highest percentage of alcohol you can find, as this is needed to preserve the stollen)

GLAZE

60 g/4 tablespoons butter, melted

1 tablespoon vanilla sugar

4 tablespoons icing/confectioners' sugar

prepared baking sheet (see page 17)

MAKES 1 STOLLEN

Day One: soaking the fruit and nuts

Put the raisins, almonds and candied peel in a bowl, cover with the alcohol and allow to soak overnight.

Day Two: making a predough and the dough

Put the flour in a bowl and make a well. Add the yeast and sugar to the well and pour in the milk. Flick some flour on the milk to close the well. Cover and allow to rest for 1 hour. After 1 hour, it will be foamy and bubbling through the top of the well. If it is not, check for signs of life by simply digging through the flour on top of the well.

Sprinkle the salt around the edge of the flour, then add the lard and lemon zest to the well. Mix and then knead well for 10 minutes – see page 12 for instructions on kneading. Now add the butter and knead again for 10 minutes until the butter is fully incorporated.

Pop it back in the bowl, cover with a tea towel and allow to rest for 30 minutes.

Gently knead the soaked fruit mixture into the dough. It will look impossible but you can do it. The raisins have a habit of jumping out of the dough and onto the floor, so watch out! [1]

Pop it back in the bowl, cover again and allow to rest for 45 minutes. Pull the dough out onto a floured surface.

Shaping

Gently stretch the dough into a rectangle 2.5 cm/1 inch thick and then fold it up as you would a piece of paper to go into an envelope: fold the bottom edge two-thirds of the way up the rectangle and gently lay it down, then stretch the top edge away from the dough and fold it right over the top of the dough, placing it gently down. Using a scraper, transfer the dough to the prepared baking sheet. Cover again and allow to rest for 30 minutes.

Preheat the oven to 240°C (475°F) Gas 9.

Pop the stollen in the preheated oven and immediately lower the temperature to 180°C (350°F) Gas 4. Bake for 50 minutes, covering it with foil after 45 minutes if the top is beginning to burn.

Remove the stollen from the oven. Place a sheet of foil on a wire rack. Carefully transfer the stollen from the baking sheet by picking it up – paper and all – and placing it on the foil. To glaze, brush half the melted butter over the warm stollen. Sprinkle on the vanilla sugar. Using a small sieve/strainer, dust on half the icing/confectioners' sugar. Spoon on the remaining melted butter (if you brush it on you will brush off all the icing/confectioners' sugar). [2]

Dust on the remaining icing/confectioners' sugar. [3]

Allow the stollen to cool completely. [4]

Wrap the stollen tightly in the paper and foil and store it at room temperature for at least 6 weeks before eating it. Invite friends round on a winter's afternoon and serve it with tea or coffee for instant cheer.

semlor

Semlor is a delicious treat, eaten all over the Nordic countries and prepared for Shrove Tuesday. Filled with fantastic rich goodness, these buns, like pancakes, were made to use up all the butter, cream, eggs and sugar in the house, ready for the fasting of Lent. Why have pancakes when you can have these? Easy to make and brilliant to eat, these buns don't keep so – such a shame – you have to eat them all up in one go! Cut them in half and fill them with marzipan and sweet, whipped cream, and invite some friends round! Signe Johansen, who has a wonderful blog called Scandilicious, generously gave me her semlor recipe, which I have adapted only slightly.

500 g/4 cups plain/all-purpose white wheat flour

2.5 g/1¼ teaspoons instant yeast, 5 g/1¾ teaspoons dry yeast, or 10 g/⅜ cake fresh yeast

75 g/⅓ cup plus 1 tablespoon sugar

250 g/1 cup milk, heated up to boiling point, then cooled to room temperature (see page 11)

8 g/2 teaspoons salt

1½ teaspoons ground cardamom seeds

50 g/3 tablespoons butter

1 egg lightly beaten with 1 tablespoon water, to glaze

marzipan and sweetened whipped cream, to serve

prepared baking sheet (see page 17)

MAKES 15

Making a predough
Put the flour in a bowl and make a well. Add the yeast and sugar to the well and pour in the milk. Flick some flour on the milk to close the well. Cover and allow to rest for 1 hour. After 1 hour, it will be foamy and bubbling through the top of the well. If it is not, check for signs of life by simply digging through the flour on top of the well.

Making the dough
Sprinkle the salt around the edge of the flour, then add the cardamom and butter to the well. Mix and then knead well for 10 minutes – see page 12 for instructions on kneading. Pop the dough back in the bowl, cover with a tea towel, shower hat or plastic bag (see page 14) and allow to rest for 2–4 hours until doubled in size. You can also let it rest in the fridge for 8–12 hours.

Pull the dough out onto an unfloured surface.

Shaping
Divide the dough into 15 portions and form into tight balls. Place them 2 cm/¾ inch apart on the prepared baking sheet. Cover with a tea towel and allow to rise until doubled in size – 1 hour if the dough is warm, or 2 hours if cold. Preheat the oven to 220°C (425°F) Gas 7.

Glaze the tops with the egg wash and bake in the preheated oven for 15–20 minutes. Remove from the oven and allow to cool completely on a wire rack. Slice them open and fill them with a layer of marzipan topped with whipped cream.

European Easter bread

All over the world, there are many different kinds of Easter bread. As Easter is the most important date in the Christian calendar, its bread is understandably special: very rich, elaborately decorated, and served reverently to friends and family. There are many varieties and shapes but all of them have certain things in common: eggs, milk, sugar and butter; marzipan and apricot glaze; poppy seeds. Some people don't like poppy seeds because they get in their teeth so I have made these optional (although I love them). Other people don't like marzipan but that is not an option at all, I am afraid!

Easter bread is fiddly so do read the recipe carefully from top to bottom before you begin. It is, however, worth every little step. Plain, this bread is great. Toasted with butter, it is sensational.

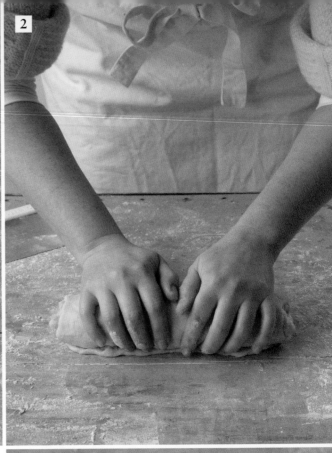

One of the fascinating things about travelling around in Europe is the seasonality of the food – and this includes most bread. With the exception of hot cross buns and panettone (both available year round, sadly) you will never see this celebration bread in a store outside its season. This means only one thing: eat it while you can – in quantity. Or bake it yourself whenever you want!

500 g/4 cups plain/all-purpose white wheat flour

2.5 g/1¼ teaspoons instant yeast, 5 g/1¾ teaspoons dry yeast, or 10 g/⅜ cake fresh yeast

75 g/⅓ cup plus 1 tablespoon sugar

250 g/1 cup milk, heated up to boiling point, then cooled to room temperature (see page 11)

4 g/1 teaspoon salt

1 teaspoon vanilla extract

3 eggs

75 g/5 tablespoons butter, at room temperature and cubed

400 g/14 oz. marzipan, grated or finely chopped

2 tablespoons apricot jam, plus a further 2 tablespoons thinned with a little water

generous handful of poppy seeds (optional)

2 small loaf pans, well greased

MAKES 2 SMALL LOAVES

Making a predough

Put the flour in a bowl and make a well. Add the yeast and sugar to the well and pour in the milk. Flick some flour on the milk to close the well. Cover and allow to rest for 1 hour. After 1 hour, it will be foamy and bubbling through the top of the well. If it is not, check for signs of life by simply digging through the flour on top of the well.

Making the dough

Sprinkle the salt around the edge of the flour, then add the vanilla and 1 egg to the well. Mix and then knead well for 10 minutes – see page 12 for instructions on kneading. Now add the butter and knead again for 10 minutes until the butter is fully incorporated.

Pop the dough back in the bowl, cover with a tea towel, shower hat or plastic bag (see page 14) and allow to rest for 2 hours until doubled in size.

Meanwhile, mix the marzipan and 2 tablespoons of apricot jam. Separate the remaining 2 eggs, reserving both the yolks and the whites. Add 2 egg whites to the marzipan mixture and beat with an electric whisk until thoroughly mixed.

Pull the dough out onto a floured surface.

Shaping

Divide the dough into 2 equal portions. Using a floured rolling pin, roll each portion into a rectangle whose width is slightly less than the length of each loaf pan. The dough should be about 1 cm/½ inch thick.

Spread half the marzipan mixture evenly and gently over each rectangle, leaving a 2-cm/¾-inch border all around the edge. [1]

If you are using poppy seeds, sprinkle the marzipan liberally with them. Add 1 teaspoon water to the reserved egg yolks, beat, and, using a spoon or a brush, apply the mixture all around the bare borders of the rectangles.

Roll the dough rectangles up into sausages, stretching gently toward you as you roll to achieve a tight sausage. [2]

Place each sausage, seam side down, on the table. Using a sharp knife, make an incision 2.5 cm/1 inch deep down the length of the sausage leaving about 2.5 cm/1 inch at both ends that is not cut. Pick up the dough and twist it a couple of times.

Place the loaf into the prepared loaf pan. [3]

Cover with a tea towel and allow to rise for 45 minutes. Preheat the oven to 170°C (325°F) Gas 3.

Glaze the loaves with the remaining egg mixture and bake in the preheated oven for 45 minutes, covering the loaves if necessary after 30 minutes to prevent them from getting too brown. Remove from the oven and transfer to a wire rack. Glaze the loaves with the remaining apricot jam while they are still hot.

kringel

500 g/4 cups plain/all-purpose
white wheat flour

2.5 g/1¼ teaspoons instant
yeast, 5 g/1¼ teaspoons dry
yeast, or 10 g/⅜ cake fresh yeast

100 g/½ cup sugar

250 g/1 cup milk, heated up to
boiling point, then cooled to
room temperature (see page 11)

1 whole egg plus 1 egg white

1 teaspoon vanilla extract

10 g/2½ teaspoons salt

1 teaspoon mixed/apple pie
spice

grated zest of 1 large lemon

100 g/6½ tablespoons butter, at
room temperature and cubed

FILLING

150 g/1 cup dried apricots

400 g/2 cups ground almonds

1 teaspoon vanilla extract

100 g/¾ cup poppy seeds

5–10 tablespoons icing/
confectioners' sugar (add it
gradually to taste)

1 egg yolk

pinch of salt

DECORATION

1 egg lightly beaten with
1 tablespoon water, to glaze

3 tablespoons poppy seeds

2 tablespoons apricot jam
thinned with a little water

*prepared baking sheet
(see page 17)*

ribbon, to decorate

SERVES 30!

*A version of this bread is made all over Germany and Eastern
Europe, especially at Easter. It comes in many shapes – fancy twists,
braids, braids made into wreaths, little buns baked in a ring… the
list goes on and on depending on where you are from and what your
family tradition is. It is essentially a 'bun dough' (ie. an enriched
bread dough) made even nicer with the addition of marzipan, poppy
seeds and an apricot glaze.*

*The Estonians, for one, make this bread to celebrate any occasion.
I received a version of this recipe from a close family friend, Maia
Matsoo. She makes it for my father whenever there is something to
celebrate. He declares it 'double yum'.*

Put the apricots for the filling in a bowl and just cover with warm
water (or the alcohol of your choice) to soften them. Allow them to
soak for 1 hour or overnight, if you like.

Making a predough
Put the flour in a bowl and make a well. Add the yeast and sugar to
the well and pour in the milk. Flick some flour on the milk to close
the well. Cover and allow to rest for 1 hour. After 1 hour, it will be
foamy and bubbling through the top of the well. If it is not, check for
signs of life by simply digging through the flour on top of the well.

Making the dough
Sprinkle the salt around the edge of the flour, then add the whole
egg, egg white, vanilla, spice and lemon zest to the well. Mix and
then knead for 10 minutes – see page 12 for instructions on kneading.
Now add the butter and knead again for 10 minutes until the butter
is fully incorporated. The dough will be sticky but don't be tempted
to add more flour.

Pop the dough back in the bowl, cover with a tea towel, shower
hat or plastic bag (see page 14) and allow to rest for 2–4 hours until
doubled in size. You can also let it rest in the fridge for 8–12 hours –
it is easier to handle when it is cold.

Meanwhile, make the filling. Drain the apricots well, squeezing out
the excess liquid, and put them in a food processor with all the other
ingredients. Whizz them to make a paste.

Pull the dough out onto a floured surface.

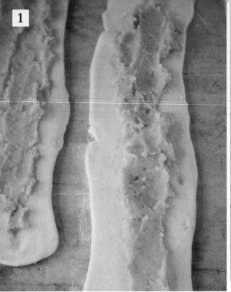

Shaping

Divide the dough into 3 equal portions and roll into loose balls. Using a floury rolling pin, roll each ball into a long rectangle about 10 cm/ 4 inches wide and ½ cm/¼ inch thick. Lay these pieces side by side on the counter.

Dot the filling all the way down the middle of each strip of dough with the help of 2 spoons. Leave a generous bare border around the edges. [1]

Using a spoon or a brush, apply a little water all around the bare borders of the strips. Fold each strip over longways and seal well to make marzipan-filled ropes.

Take the 3 ropes and braid them together. [2]

Bend the braid into a wreath, pinch the edges of the braid together and seal them well. [3]

Carefully slide the wreath onto the prepared baking sheet. Cover with a tea towel and allow to rest until doubled in size – 1–2 hours if the dough is warm, or 2–4 hours if the dough is cold.

Preheat the oven to 180°C (350°F) Gas 4.

To decorate, glaze the kringel with the egg wash and scatter the poppy seeds on top. Bake in the preheated oven for 45 minutes until deep golden, covering with foil after 30 minutes to prevent it from getting too brown.

Remove from the oven and transfer to a wire rack. Brush the apricot jam solution over the kringel while it is still hot.

Allow to cool completely, then wrap a lovely ribbon around the untidy, sealed part of the wreath where the 3 ends of the braid join together. Make sure people don't eat the ribbon in their greedy feeding frenzy.

tsoureki

In Greece, they celebrate Easter with this splendid bread. As with any country and any kind of bread, there are many different variations, the most spectacular of which has an entire hard-boiled egg, dyed deep red, inserted into the dough before it is baked! It is beautiful but it is an option. My lovely neighbour, Dimitrios Alexiou, gave me his recipe for Greek Easter Bread.

You can find gum mastic and mahlepi/mahleb from a Greek store where you can also buy the red dye for the egg if you cannot buy it anywhere else.

35 g/2½ tablespoons sheep butter plus 35 g/2½ tablespoons (cow) butter, or simply 70 g/5 tablespoons (cow) butter

150 g/⅔ cup milk

160 g/¾ cup sugar

5 g/1 big teaspoon ground gum mastic (optional)

5 g/2 teaspoons mahlepi/mahleb (ground Rock cherry kernels) (optional)

3 eggs

650 g/5 cups plain/all-purpose white wheat flour

3.5 g/1¾ teaspoons instant yeast, 7 g/2¼ teaspoons dry yeast, or 14 g/⅞ cake fresh yeast

14 g/3½ teaspoons salt

DECORATION

1 egg lightly beaten with 1 tablespoon water

flaked/slivered almonds

prepared baking sheet (see page 17)

hard-boiled egg, dyed red (optional)

MAKES 1 LARGE LOAF

Making a predough

Put the butter, milk, sugar, gum mastic and mahlepi/mahleb in a saucepan and heat gently until the butter has melted completely and the milk is just below boiling point. Stir constantly to make sure it does not burn. Remove from the heat, pour it into a big bowl, then allow to cool completely.

Add the eggs to the cooled liquid and mix well.

Put the flour in a bowl and make a well. Add the yeast to the well and pour in the milk mixture. Flick some flour on the milk to close the well. Cover and allow to rest for 1 hour. After 1 hour, it will be foamy and bubbling through the top of the well. If it is not, check for signs of life by simply digging through the flour on top of the well.

Making the dough

Sprinkle the salt around the edge of the flour, then mix everything together. Knead well for 10 minutes – see page 12 for instructions on kneading.

Pop the dough back in the bowl, cover with a tea towel, shower hat or plastic bag (see page 14) and allow to rest for 2–4 hours until doubled in size. You can also let it rest in the fridge for 8–12 hours.

Pull the dough out onto a floured surface.

Shaping

Divide the dough into 3 equal portions. Roll each portion into a rope about 2.5 cm/1 inch thick. Make a braid, then cover with a dry tea towel and allow to rest for 2 hours.

If you are using the red egg, gently press the egg at an angle toward one end of the loaf. Cover again and allow to rest for 1 hour.

Preheat the oven to 180°C (350°F) Gas 4.

To decorate, glaze the tsoureki with the egg wash and scatter flaked/slivered almonds on top. Bake in the preheated oven for 1 hour until golden, covering with foil after 45 minutes to prevent it from getting too brown. Remove from the oven and transfer to a wire rack.

challah

Challah is baked to celebrate the Jewish Sabbath and holidays. It is an enriched bread, decorated with seeds that represent the manna that fell from heaven, and it comes in many shapes, all of which have a specific meaning. Whatever your faith, challah is delicious, beautiful and easy to make. It is never cut with a knife. To share challah, you pass it and break it by hand.

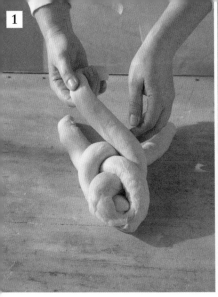

500 g/4 cups plain/all-purpose white wheat flour

2.5 g/1¼ teaspoons instant yeast, 5 g/1¾ teaspoons dry yeast, or 10 g/⅜ cake fresh yeast

50 g/¼ cup sugar

200 g/¾ cup water

10 g/2½ teaspoons salt

2 eggs

2 tablespoons vegetable oil, butter or chicken fat, depending on what else you are eating

DECORATION

1 egg lightly beaten with 1 tablespoon water, to glaze

poppy, sesame and/or nigella seeds

large loaf pan, greased, or prepared baking sheet (see page 17)

MAKES 1 LARGE LOAF

Making a predough

Put the flour in a bowl and make a well. Add the yeast and sugar to the well and pour in the water. Flick some flour on the water to close the well. Cover and allow to rest for 1 hour. After 1 hour, it will be foamy and bubbling through the top of the well. If it is not, check for signs of life by simply digging through the flour on top of the well.

Making the dough

Sprinkle the salt around the edge of the flour, then add the eggs and fat to the well. Mix and then knead well for 10 minutes – see page 12 for instructions on kneading.

Pop the dough back in the bowl, cover with a tea towel, shower hat or plastic bag (see page 14) and allow to rest for 2 hours until doubled in size.

Pull the dough out onto a floured surface.

Shaping

Divide the dough into 3 equal portions. Roll each portion into a long rope about 2 cm/¾ inch thick. Pinch the ends of all 3 together to fasten them. Now braid them. [1]

When you have finished braiding, pinch the ends together to seal, then tuck them neatly underneath the braid. [2]

Place the braid inside the prepared loaf pan or on a prepared baking sheet, cover again and allow to rest for 1 hour. Preheat the oven to 200°C (400°F) Gas 6.

To decorate, glaze the challah with the egg wash and scatter the seeds on top. [3]

Bake in the preheated oven for 45 minutes until golden brown. Remove from the oven and transfer to a wire rack.

Variations: Replace the sugar with honey. You can also add raisins or other dried fruit to make the challah even more special and festive.

pan de muerto

Celebration bread would have come over to Mexico with the Spanish, to celebrate the key dates in the Catholic calendar. The Mexicans have a way of adapting things to their ways and infusing them with charm, and this bread is no exception. Made for All Souls Day, it comes with dough 'bones' draped on the outside to look like skeletons, and little dough-ball 'skulls' on top.

500 g/4 cups plain/all-purpose white wheat flour

2.5 g/1¼ teaspoons instant yeast, 5 g/1¼ teaspoons dry yeast, or 10 g/⅝ cake fresh yeast

120 g/1 cup plus 2 tablespoons sugar

50 g/3 tablespoons water

10 g/2½ teaspoons salt

5 eggs

½ teaspoon orange flower water

½ teaspoon ground anise

2 tablespoons orange juice

200 g/13 tablespoons butter, at room temperature and cubed, plus extra, melted, to glaze

GLAZE

1 egg, lightly beaten

1 tablespoon water

½ tablespoon sugar

½ teaspoon salt

DECORATION

75 g/½ cup melted butter

200 g/1 cup sugar

prepared baking sheet (see page 17)

MAKES 4 SMALL LOAVES

Making a predough
Put the flour in a bowl and make a well. Add the yeast and sugar to the well and pour in the water. Flick some flour on the water to close the well. Cover and allow to rest for 1 hour. After 1 hour, it will be foamy and bubbling through the top of the well. If it is not, check for signs of life by simply digging through the flour on top of the well.

Making the dough
Sprinkle the salt around the edge of the flour, then add the eggs, orange flower water, anise and orange juice to the well. Mix and then knead well for 10 minutes – see page 12 for instructions on kneading.

Now add the butter and knead again for 10–20 minutes until the butter is fully incorporated. Don't panic! The dough will get very slack but it will firm up again.

Scrape the dough back into the bowl, cover with clingfilm/plastic wrap and allow to rest until doubled in size – 12 hours in the fridge or 6 hours at room temperature.

Pull the dough out onto a floured surface.

Shaping
Divide the dough into 4 equal portions, then pinch a 50-g/2-oz. piece off each one. Set these little pieces aside. Shape the bigger portions into 4 tight balls and place them on the prepared baking sheet. These are your 'bodies'. Now turn to the little pieces of dough. Pinch about one-third off each of them and roll these into 4 little balls. These are your 'skulls'. Divide the remaining two-thirds of the little pieces of dough into 4 small pieces and roll each piece into sausages. These are your 'bones'. You should have 4 bones and 1 skull for each body.

Make the glaze by mixing together the egg, water, sugar and salt and painting each body. Stick the skulls on top of each body and the bones in a criss-cross pattern down the sides.

Cover with a dry tea towel and allow to rise until doubled in size – 2 hours if the dough is warm, or 4 hours if the dough is cold. Preheat the oven to 220°C (425°F) Gas 7.

Bake the bread in the preheated oven for 20 minutes until it sounds hollow when tapped. Remove from the oven and transfer to a wire rack. To decorate, brush it with the melted butter and dust liberally with the sugar.

Celebrate in Mexico
– with wheat and maize

'Sin maíz, no hay país' – 'no corn, no country' – sums up the importance of corn in Mexico. Although wheat has been cultivated there for more than 500 years, the truly representative grain is corn. No bread on the table? No drama. No corn tortillas on the table? Probable drama. Corn and life are the same.

Corn tortillas are not considered to be flat bread. They are tortillas, a separate food category, and they are eaten in many forms – both simply and elegantly – and the list of what is made out of them is endless. Maize flour, the main ingredient in a corn tortilla, is also used to make tamales, savoury and sweet pies and cakes, and even drinks. Corn is the indigenous grain and is still eaten by everyone on a daily basis.

Wheat is a modern addition to the Mexican diet, and is part of the story of economic and social control by the Spanish who began milling wheat in 1521, just three years after the conquests ended. By the 1700s, thousands of bakeries all over Mexico had opened up making sweet bread – pan dulce – that is still sold today.

Originally, the practice of baking bread rolls enabled bakers to express themselves artistically and allowed poor people to buy their own small 'loaf' rather than being forced to buy slices of bread off a bigger loaf which go stale quickly

and are less dignified to purchase. Today it is all about tradition and choice. In a typical Mexican bakery, and even in the bakery section of a supermarket, you select exactly what you want before going to the till to pay and see your purchases wrapped up in a beautiful package. Mexicans eat 'pan dulce' any time of day with a hot drink such as coffee, hot chocolate or 'atole'.

Today, the number of small bakeries and independent tortilla makers is on the decline. The rise in the power of the supermarkets, the availability of extremely cheap, industrially made bread and tortillas, and the quest for convenience – three global trends that harm the quality of bread consumed in almost every country in the world – have come to Mexico. Sadly, it is no longer easy to buy good bread or tortillas on every street corner and it is almost impossible to buy good quality flour – be it maize or wheat.

rosca de reyes

In Spanish, a 'rosca' is a wreath and 'reyes' means kings. The 'rosca de reyes', therefore, is a wreath of the kings and is baked in Mexico to mark Epiphany on the 6 January, when the three kings presented gifts to the Christ child in the stable. This is a delicious, enriched bread full of eggs and butter but it goes one better: the top of the bread is lavishly decorated with candied fruit and inside the bread the baker hides a little token or a tiny model of Baby Jesus. Whoever gets the token hosts a party on 2 February (the day Christ was presented at the temple) where tamales are served. Versions of this bread are made all over the world to celebrate Epiphany – such as the 'galette des rois' in France – and while the shapes change, they all seem to feature a token in the middle.

500 g/4 cups plain/all-purpose white wheat flour

2.5 g/1¼ teaspoons instant yeast, 5 g/1¾ teaspoons dry yeast, or 10 g/⅜ cake fresh yeast

120 g/1 cup plus 2 tablespoons sugar, plus extra for dusting

50 ml/3 tablespoons water

10 g/2½ teaspoons salt

5 eggs

1 teaspoon orange flower water

200 g/13 tablespoons butter, at room temperature and cubed, plus extra, melted, to glaze

DECORATION

1 egg, lightly beaten

1 tablespoon water

½ tablespoon sugar, plus extra to sprinkle

½ teaspoon salt

candied fruit, eg. angelica, pears, plums, orange, lemon, cherries or anything bright and cheerful

2 prepared baking sheets (see page 17)

2 tokens or statues

MAKES 2 MEDIUM LOAVES

Making a predough

Put the flour in a bowl and make a well. Add the yeast and sugar to the well and pour in the water. Flick some flour on the water to close the well. Cover and allow to rest for 1 hour. After 1 hour, it will be foamy and bubbling through the top of the well. If it is not, check for signs of life by simply digging through the flour on top of the well.

Making the dough

Sprinkle the salt around the edge of the flour, then add the eggs and orange flower water to the well. Mix and then knead well for 10 minutes – see page 12 for instructions on kneading.

Now add the butter and knead again for 10–20 minutes until the butter is fully incorporated. Don't panic! The dough will get very slack but it will firm up again.

Scrape the dough back into the bowl, cover with clingfilm/plastic wrap and allow to rest until doubled in size – 12 hours in the fridge or 6 hours at room temperature.

Pull the dough out onto a floured surface.

Shaping

Divide the dough in 2 and shape into tight balls. Cover with a tea towel and allow to rest for 15 minutes until they soften up a bit.

Poke a hole through the middle of each ball with the handle of a utensil. See [picture 1], overleaf.

Gently widen the dough with your hands and with gravity to expand it into a ring. See [picture 2], overleaf.

The dough making the ring should be about 6 cm/2½ inches wide. Place the rings on the prepared baking sheets. Push the token or statue up into the dough from beneath.

To decorate, make a glaze by mixing together the egg, water, sugar and salt. Paint it over the rings with a pastry brush. Sprinkle sugar thickly over the tops of the rings in 4–6 stripes – 3 cm/ 1½ inches wide – spaced evenly around each ring. Between the sugar stripes, arrange your choice of candied fruit. [3]

Cover with a tea towel and allow to rise until doubled in size – 2 hours if the dough is warm, or 4 hours if the dough is cold.

Preheat the oven to 180°C (350°F) Gas 4.

Bake the rings in the preheated oven for 30 minutes or until the bread is golden on the top. Remove from the oven and transfer to a wire rack.

savoury christmas bread

This bread, made with wheat flour, would have been brought over with the Spaniards, Italians and Portuguese when they settled in South America. Although it is a Christmas bread made with all sorts of goodies that would have had to have come by boat from a very long way away, you can now make it any time and it is a fantastic bread to have at a party or on a picnic because it looks impressive and is an easy way to eat lots of treats all at once!

600 g/4¾ cups strong white (bread) flour

350 g/1½ cups water

50 g/3 tablespoons olive oil

3 g/1½ teaspoons instant yeast, 6 g/2 teaspoons dry yeast, or 12 g/¾ cake fresh yeast

12 g/1 tablespoon salt

FILLING

olive oil, for brushing

about 12 slices of lovely ham

about 12 slices of tasty cheese, eg. manchego, gruyère, havarti

about 20 slices of delicious salami

20 green and/or black pitted olives

couple of pinches of dried mixed herbs

freshly ground black pepper

prepared baking sheet (see page 17)

MAKES 2 LARGE LOAVES

If you are using instant or fresh yeast, put all the ingredients in a big bowl and mix them together. Tip out onto the counter and knead well for 10 minutes – see page 12 for instructions on kneading.

If you are using dry yeast, put the flour in a big bowl and make a well. Add the dry yeast to the well and pour in 100 g/½ cup of the water. Cover and allow to rest for 15 minutes. You may or may not get a beige sludge on the top of the water, but don't worry – what is important is to dissolve the yeast. Add the rest of the ingredients and mix. Tip out onto the counter and knead well for 10 minutes – see page 12 for instructions on kneading.

Pop the kneaded dough back into the bowl and cover with a tea towel, shower hat or plastic bag (see page 14). Allow to rest for 1–2 hours until doubled in size.

Pull the dough out onto a floured surface.

Shaping

Divide the dough into 2 equal portions and roll into rectangles about 1 cm/¾ inch thick and with one edge measuring 30–40 cm/12–16 inches. Brush the dough all over with olive oil and then lay down one layer of ham, one layer of cheese and one layer of salami, in any order, leaving a 1-cm/½-inch border all around. Scatter the olives and herbs over the top and then grind fresh pepper on top of the whole thing.

Roll up each rectangle tightly so that it feels as firm as possible and seal the edges. Place them, seam side down, on the prepared baking sheet. Cover with a dry tea towel and allow to rest for 1 hour. Preheat the oven to 200°C (400°F) Gas 6.

Brush olive oil over the loaves and, using a sharp knife, make 4–5 incisions about 2.5 cm/1 inch deep to allow the bread to expand while it bakes. Bake in the preheated oven for 45 minutes. Remove from the oven and transfer to a wire rack.

sweet bread

Sweet bread, also called coffee bread, buns or pan dulce, makes a wonderful alternative to cake. You can find different kinds of sweet bread all over the world and it is delicious when eaten with a hot drink as a light meal or a snack. It is easy to bake and beautiful to look at – making any occasion special and memorable. It takes a little bit more time than cake but try it sometime for a change – I am sure you, your friends and your family will be delighted.

chelsea buns

The English have great buns. Many different kinds of buns are sold at every good bakery and they are extremely satisfying with a cup of strong tea. Chelsea buns are stuffed with dried fruit and shaped into a beautiful swirly shape – fantastic for gradually unravelling and nibbling on. Does anybody know if they actually come from Chelsea?

300 g/2¼ cups plain/all-purpose white wheat flour

200 g/¾ cup water

1.5 g/¾ teaspoon instant yeast, 3 g/1 teaspoon dry yeast, or 6 g/⅛ cake fresh yeast

6 g/1½ teaspoons salt

1 tablespoon butter

1 tablespoon sugar

FILLING

75 g/½ cup dried fruit, raisins, sultanas/golden raisins, currants or a mixture

25 g/2½ tablespoons dried orange or lemon or mixed peel

50 g/¼ cup packed soft brown sugar or demerara

25 g/2 tablespoons butter, melted and cooled

2 big tablespoons honey, melted, to glaze

deep baking pan, about 25 cm/10 inches wide, well greased

MAKES 8–10

If you are using instant or fresh yeast, put all the ingredients in a big bowl and mix them together. Tip out onto the counter and knead well for 10 minutes – see page 12 for instructions on kneading.

If you are using dry yeast, put the flour in a big bowl and make a well. Add the dry yeast to the well and pour in 100 g/½ cup of the water. Cover and allow to rest for 15 minutes. You may or may not get a beige sludge on the top of the water, but don't worry – what is important is to dissolve the yeast. Add the rest of the ingredients and mix. Tip out onto the counter and knead well for 10 minutes – see page 12 for instructions on kneading.

Pop the kneaded dough back into the bowl and cover with a tea towel, shower hat or plastic bag (see page 14). Allow to rest for 1–2 hours until doubled in size.

Meanwhile, mix the dried fruit, peel and sugar together to make the filling. Put it in a little bowl and set it aside.

Pull the dough out onto a well-floured surface.

Shaping

Using a rolling pin, roll the dough into a rectangle about 30 x 23 cm/12 x 9 inches. Brush the cooled, melted butter over it and scatter the fruit mixture evenly over the top.

Roll up the rectangle, tugging it gently toward you at each roll to achieve a tight sausage. If you want to cover it and place it in the fridge for 30 minutes or so at this stage, please do – it makes it easier to slice.

Use a sharp, serrated knife to cut the sausage into 8–10 slices if you like your buns thin, or 6 slices if you like them really fat. Place them in the prepared baking pan. They can be snuggled in tightly if you want them to rise up or left with plenty of room between them if you want them to spread out. Place a tea towel over the pan – its deep sides prevent the towel from sticking to the buns. If you don't have a pan with deep sides, lightly flour the tea towel before placing it over the buns. Allow to rest for 1 hour until doubled in size.

Preheat the oven to 180°C (350°F) Gas 4.

Bake the buns in the preheated oven for 30–35 minutes until golden. Remove from the oven and transfer to a wire rack. Brush the buns with melted honey while they are still hot.

bath buns

Do bath buns come from Bath any more than chelsea buns come from Chelsea? I have no idea, so get in touch if you have the answer! One of the things I love about bath buns is their shape: they are simply blobbed onto the baking sheet to be baked. No fancy rolling. Every bun is different and even a toddler can do it. The other thing I love about them is that you can sit for a long time and contentedly lick the sugar from the tops of these buns while you drink your tea. It's kind of disgusting though so you may not want to do it in public.

500 g/4 cups plain/all-purpose white wheat flour

2.5 g/1¼ teaspoons instant yeast, 5 g/1¾ teaspoons dry yeast, or 10 g/⅜ cake fresh yeast

50 g/¼ cup sugar

250 g/1 cup milk, heated up to boiling point, then cooled to room temperature (see page 11)

10 g/2½ teaspoons salt

50 g/3 tablespoons butter

2 eggs

150 g/1 cup sultanas/golden raisins

50 g/⅓ cup mixed candied peel

rock/coarse sugar, to sprinkle

deep roasting dish lined with parchment paper

MAKES ABOUT 12

Making a predough
Put the flour in a big bowl and make a well. Add the yeast and sugar to the well and pour in the milk. Flick some flour on the milk to close the well. Cover and allow to rest for 1 hour. After 1 hour, it will be foamy and bubbling through the top of the well. If it is not, check for signs of life by simply digging through the flour on top of the well.

Making the dough
Sprinkle the salt around the edge of the flour, then add the butter and eggs to the well. Mix and then knead well for 10 minutes – see page 12 for instructions on kneading.

Pop it back in the bowl, cover with a tea towel and allow to rest for 15 minutes.

Gently knead the sultanas/golden raisins and peel into the dough. Pop the dough back in the bowl, cover with a tea towel, shower hat or plastic bag (see page 14) and allow to rest for 2 hours until doubled in size.

Shaping
Pull the dough out of the bowl and spoon 12 blobs onto the prepared roasting dish. Sprinkle rock/coarse sugar liberally over each blob. Place a tea towel over the dish – its deep sides prevent the towel from sticking to the buns. If you don't have a pan with deep sides, lightly flour the tea towel before placing it over the buns. Allow to rest for 1 hour until doubled in size.

Preheat the oven to 180°C (350°F) Gas 4.

Bake the buns in the preheated oven for 20 minutes until golden and they sound hollow when tapped. Remove from the oven and transfer to a wire rack.

aniseed bread

There are recipes for aniseed bread all over the world – it's truly amazing. How did this spice make it everywhere? Some aniseed bread is hard and crunchy and not made with any yeast at all; some is simply basic bread with aniseed mixed into the dough; some is enriched; some is flat. And there are endless varieties of shapes and sizes. I have provided one recipe here which comes from Spain, but there is no reason why you cannot vary the recipe or the shape as you please. Send in your variations – I love to read recipes and adore to look at photos.

This is a sweet bread, but if you would like to make it savoury, simply omit the sugar. I like to eat it with butter for tea, or altogether plain with a lovely dry sherry as a little pre-dinner snack.

2 tablespoons butter

400 g/3 cups strong white (bread) flour

2 g/1 teaspoon instant yeast, 4 g/1¼ teaspoons dry yeast, or 8 g/½ cake fresh yeast

250 g/1 cup water

8 g/2 teaspoons salt

50 g/¼ cup sugar

2 tablespoons whole anise seeds

1 egg

GLAZE

1 egg yolk

1 tablespoon water

1 tablespoon sugar

2 proofing baskets, well floured, and a prepared baking sheet; or 2 small loaf pans, greased (see page 17)

MAKES 2 SMALL LOAVES

Melt the butter in a small saucepan and allow to cool while you make the dough.

If you are using instant or fresh yeast, put all the ingredients in a big bowl and mix them together. Tip out onto the counter and knead well for 10 minutes – see page 12 for instructions on kneading.

If you are using dry yeast, put the flour in a big bowl and make a well. Sprinkle the dry yeast in the well and add 100 g/½ cup of the water. Cover and allow to rest for 15 minutes. You may or may not get a beige sludge on the top of the water, but don't worry – what is important is to dissolve the yeast. Add the rest of the ingredients and mix. Tip out onto the counter and knead well for 10 minutes – see page 12 for instructions on kneading.

Scrape the melted butter into the bowl and pop the kneaded dough back on top of it. Coat the dough well with the butter and then cover with a tea towel, shower hat or plastic bag (see page 14). Allow to rest for 1–2 hours until doubled in size.

Pull the dough out onto an unfloured surface.

Shaping

Divide the dough into 2 equal portions, cover with a tea towel and allow to rest for 10 minutes.

Roll each portion into a tight ball or sausage and pop it into the prepared proofing baskets or loaf pans. Cover with a tea towel and allow to rest for 1 hour.

Preheat the oven to 220°C (425°F) Gas 7.

If proofing in baskets, carefully turn the dough out onto the prepared baking sheet. If baking in pans, leave the dough in the pans. To glaze, mix together the egg yolk, water and sugar and paint it on the loaves.

Bake in the preheated oven for 30 minutes until deep brown. To check whether they are done, tap the bottoms of the loaves. If they sound hollow, they are done. If not, pop them back for another 5 minutes or so, until they do. Remove from the oven and transfer to a wire rack.

Explore Germany
The widest variety of bread

Germany has around 2,600 unique recipes for bread and it looks as if, for this reason, German bread will soon be included on the UNESCO 'intangible cultural heritage' list. They deserve it. German bread is fantastic both for its variety and its quality. Many German bakers whose loaves are sold out day after day nevertheless place a ceiling on their own wealth by limiting their capacity and selling only very locally. Some install tiny grain mills in their shops to ensure they have exactly the flour they want. Others bake day in and day out on portable wood-fired ovens in market places and at festivals six days a week. Still others distinguish themselves by developing new types of packaging to enable them to bag the bread while it is warm and to keep it fresh. Hundreds of bakers commit themselves to turning out the highest-quality handmade product they can.

Of course, not all bread in Germany is fantastic. Supermarkets sell sliced white 'toast bread', and fairly rubbishy breads and buns dressed up as something special are sold through chain bakeries, but even that bread seems so much better than most of the bread available in most other countries.

It is impossible to separate Germans from their bread. Ask a travelling German what they miss from home and the answer is invariably the bread, not, 'my husband, cat, bed, shower gel, beer, or sausages' – it's 'the bread'.

My German mother learned to bake bread through sheer desperation in 1950 when she left Germany for Canada. She could not find any good bread, 'the kind you have to chew.' My mother was born in Stade, a little town on the Elbe river west of Lübeck, the first 'stadt' in the Hanseatic League, a 1,000-year-old trading organization centred around the Baltic Sea.

It is the Hanseatic League that explains why towns around the Baltic are so similar. Not just the architecture and city plans, but also their café cultures, use of particular spices, and the style of the bread and cakes. All over the Baltic you find rye bread redolent with exotic spices, malt syrup and molasses; fancy buns with cinnamon and cardamom; and celebration bread with apricots, ground almonds and poppy seeds. They may have different names but they are the same thanks to the network of towns that traded spices from the east, fruit and nuts from the south, and coffee and tea from all over the world.

White bread, in my mother's opinion, is pappy stuff which sticks to the roof of your mouth and has to be prised off in a most unmannerly fashion. To my English father's delight, a German bakery opened quite close to where my parents live, which means my mother turned her hand to baking cakes instead of bread. At 82, she still makes a one-hour round trip journey to buy 10-kg rye and wheat sourdough loaves which she cuts up and puts in the freezer. My brother and I grew up on toasted sourdough soldiers for our eggs and took half-moon-shaped sandwiches to school stuffed with smoked ham, strong cheese or leberwurst. We survived to tell the tale and although we publicly longed for our friends' square, white sandwiches filled with processed cheese, bologna, or peanut butter and jelly, we were secretly glad we did not have to eat them.

cardamom knots

Cardamom is a spice that we normally associate with South Asia but it is used widely in northern Europe in both sweet and savoury bread. If you cannot find it ground or crushed you will need to split open the cardamom pods to extract the black seeds and crush or grind them yourself. I like to make these cardamom knots really small so you can just have a tiny bit of loveliness with your tea.

300 g/2⅓ cups plain/
all-purpose white wheat flour

1.5 g/¾ teaspoon instant yeast,
3 g/1 teaspoon dry yeast, or
6 g/⅜ cake fresh yeast

2 tablespoons sugar

200 g/¾ cup water

6 g/1½ teaspoons salt

1 teaspoon ground cardamom
seeds

100 g/6½ tablespoons butter, at
room temperature and cubed

FILLING

100 g/6½ tablespoons butter,
at room temperature

100 g/½ cup muscovado or
white sugar

3 tablespoons crushed
cardamom seeds

GLAZE

100 g/6½ tablespoons butter

100 g/½ cup sugar

1 tablespoon crushed
cardamom seeds

*deep roasting dishes lined with
parchment paper*

MAKES LOTS!

Making a predough
Put the flour in a big bowl and make a well. Add the yeast and sugar to the well and pour in 100 g/½ cup of the water. Flick some flour on the water to close the well. Cover and allow to rest for 1 hour. After 1 hour, it will be foamy and bubbling through the top of the well. If it is not, check for signs of life by simply digging through the flour on top of the well.

Making the dough
Sprinkle the salt around the edge of the flour, then add the rest of the water and the ground cardamom to the well. Mix and then knead well for 10 minutes – see page 12 for instructions on kneading.

Now add the butter and knead again for 10–20 minutes until the butter is fully incorporated. Don't panic! The dough will get very slack but it will firm up again.

Pop the dough back in the bowl, cover with a tea towel, shower hat or plastic bag (see page 14) and allow to rest for 2–4 hours until doubled in size. You can also let it rest in the fridge for 8–12 hours – it is easier to handle when it is cold.

Meanwhile, to make the filling, beat the butter and sugar together until very pale. Mix in the crushed cardamom seeds. Cover and set aside at room temperature until later.

Pull the dough out onto a floured surface.

Shaping
Using a rolling pin, roll the dough into a rectangle about 30 x 23 cm/ 12 x 9 inches. Spread the filling evenly over it. Fold the top edge into the middle and gently press down. Then fold the bottom edge right over the dough to the top edge – as if you were folding a letter in thirds to go into an envelope – and gently press down. Roll it again with the rolling pin until nearly back to its original size, then cut it into strips 2 cm/¾ inch wide. Twist each strip several times, then tie in a simple knot. Place in the roasting dishes, cover with a dry tea towel and allow to rise until doubled in size – 1 hour if the dough is warm, or 2 hours if the dough is cold. Preheat the oven to 220°C (425°F) Gas 7.

To make a glaze, melt the butter and stir in the sugar and crushed cardamom seeds. Let it cool slightly and brush all over the knots. Bake in the preheated oven for 20 minutes. Remove from the oven and transfer to a wire rack.

maple syrup buns

Maple syrup is a traditional sweetener in eastern Canada and the northeastern United States. Until sugar was introduced from France and England, maple syrup and maple sugar were the only sweeteners. As it is completely unrefined, it retains many of its natural nutrients.

'Sugaring off' is still a common custom all over eastern Canada and the northeastern United States. Commercially, that is when sap is collected, simmered and bottled by the large growers. Domestically, and as part of festivals, maple sugar is boiled in great kettles over fires and then drizzled over pans of snow where it freezes and makes instant candy. Pancakes, sausages, all different kinds of bread, cakes, and pies are made to celebrate this occasion every year.

2 medium potatoes

500 g/4 cups plain/all-purpose white wheat flour

2.5 g/1¼ teaspoons instant yeast, 5 g/1¾ teaspoons dry yeast, or 10 g/⅜ cake fresh yeast

2 tablespoons maple sugar (or brown sugar if you cannot get maple sugar)

250 g/1 cup milk, heated up to boiling point, then cooled to room temperature (see page 11)

2 eggs

10 g/2½ teaspoons salt

1 tablespoon ground cinnamon

2 tablespoons lard or butter

125 ml/½ cup maple syrup, to glaze

prepared baking sheets (see page 17)

MAKES 4 DOZEN BUNS

Peel the potatoes, then boil them and mash them and allow to cool completely before using for the bread dough. You can make them the night before.

Making a predough
Put the flour in a bowl and make a well. Add the yeast and sugar to the well and pour in the milk. Flick some flour on the milk to close the well. Cover and allow to rest for 1 hour. After 1 hour, it will be foamy and bubbling through the top of the well. If it is not, check for signs of life by simply digging through the flour on top of the well.

Making the dough
Lightly beat the eggs and stir them into the mashed potatoes. Mix in the salt, cinnamon, lard or butter and blend well. Add the potato mixture into the predough and mix. Pull out onto the counter and knead well for 10 minutes – see page 12 for instructions on kneading.

It will be sticky so please persevere, resisting the temptation to add more flour. After 10 minutes, pop the dough back in the bowl, cover with a tea towel, shower hat or plastic bag (see page 14) and allow to rest for 2 hours until doubled in size.

Pull the dough out onto a floured surface.

Shaping
Using a floured rolling pin, roll the dough out until about 2.5 cm/ 1 inch thick. Cut it into squares with a knife or use a cookie cutter to stamp out rounds about 5 cm/2 inches across. Place them on the prepared baking sheets, lightly flour the tops and cover with a dry tea towel. Allow to rest for 1 hour.

Preheat the oven to 220°C (425°F) Gas 7.

Bake the buns in the preheated oven for 15–20 minutes until golden brown. Remove from the oven and transfer to a wire rack.

Pour the maple syrup into a saucepan and boil until it reaches the 'thread' stage – 112°C/238°F. Drizzle it onto the buns while they are still warm.

1

2

3

People drive for miles, or ride for miles
in their little boats to buy cinnamon buns,
warm and sticky from the oven before
racing back home to eat them with a summer
breakfast of freshly picked blueberries or
newly caught trout, depending on your tastes.
Now that you can make them, you need not
leave the house at all!

cinnamon buns

Cinnamon buns remind me of trips up to cottage country, north of Toronto where I grew up. It was difficult to get them home from the bakery without eating them, which is why I always wanted to go with my dad to pick them up. He always bought two extra for us to eat secretly on the way home.

300 g/2⅓ cups plain/all-purpose white wheat flour

200 g/¾ cup water

1.5 g/¾ teaspoon instant yeast, 3 g/1 teaspoon dry yeast, or 6 g/⅛ cake fresh yeast

6 g/1½ teaspoons salt

FILLING

150 g/10 tablespoons butter, at room temperature

125 g/⅔ cup packed soft dark brown sugar or muscovado

2 big tablespoons ground cinnamon

GLAZE

150 g/10 tablespoons butter, at room temperature

125 g/⅔ cup packed soft dark brown sugar or muscovado

deep, 30 x 30-cm/12 x 12-inch roasting dish

MAKES 12

If you are using instant or fresh yeast, put all the ingredients in a big bowl and mix them together. Tip out onto the counter and knead well for 10 minutes – see page 12 for instructions on kneading.

If you are using dry yeast, put the flour in a big bowl and make a well. Add the dry yeast to the well and pour in 100 g/½ cup of the water. Cover and allow to rest for 15 minutes. You may or may not get a beige sludge on the top of the water, but don't worry – what is important is to dissolve the yeast. Add the rest of the ingredients and mix. Tip out onto the counter and knead well for 10 minutes – see page 12 for instructions on kneading.

Pop the kneaded dough back into the bowl and cover with a tea towel, shower hat or plastic bag (see page 14). Allow to rest for 1–2 hours until doubled in size.

Meanwhile, for the filling, beat everything together and set aside, and for the glaze, put the butter and sugar in a wide, shallow saucepan. Heat gently, stirring constantly to prevent it burning, until the sugar and butter are incorporated. Set aside.

Pull the dough out onto a well-floured surface.

Shaping

Using a rolling pin, roll the dough into a rectangle about 30 x 23 cm/12 x 9 inches. Spread the filling evenly over the dough. [1]

Roll up the rectangle, tugging it gently toward you at each roll to achieve a tight sausage. [2]

If you want to cover it and place it in the fridge for 30 minutes or so at this stage, please do – it makes it easier to slice. Use a sharp, serrated knife to cut the sausage into 12 slices if you like your buns thin, or 8 slices if you like them really fat. [3]

Stir the glaze. Roll each bun in the glaze, then place them in the roasting dish. Scrape the remaining glaze over them. Place a tea towel over the pan. Allow to rest for 1 hour until doubled in size. Preheat the oven to 200°C (400°F) Gas 6.

Bake the buns in the preheated oven for 40 minutes until golden brown. If they get too brown, cover them with foil. Remove from the oven and turn them out onto a plate by placing the plate on top of the pan and inverting it. Be extremely careful not to spill the hot melted glaze or you will burn yourself and waste the best bit.

Technically a cake, I have included this recipe because it is made with yeast, so I have rather decided it is a sweet bread (I can hear my grandmother laughing at me). I first ate this in Germany as a child. My grandmother filled it with poppy seeds, apples, plums, strawberries, red currants – whatever was in season and that she had in the house. If there was nothing in the house, she simply topped it with 'streusel', which means crumbs. To make more of a sweet bread, fill it with poppy seeds and crumbs; to make more of a cake, fill it with fruit and then top with whipped cream. It is my very favourite thing in the world to make with yeast.

streusel kuchen

350 g/2¾ cups plain/all-purpose white wheat flour

1.25 g/1 scant teaspoon instant yeast, 3.5 g/1 generous teaspoon dry yeast, or 6 g/⅛ cake fresh yeast

150 g/⅔ cup milk, heated up to boiling point, then cooled to room temperature (see page 11)

4 egg yolks

75 g/6 tablespoons sugar

5 g/1¼ teaspoons salt

75 g/5 tablespoons butter, at room temperature

OPTION ONE: POPPY-SEED FILLING

500 g/2 cups milk

1 tablespoon vanilla sugar

grated zest of 1 lemon

1 tablespoon custard powder

500 g/4 cups poppy seeds, crushed or ground slightly with a mortar and pestle, or a clean coffee/spice grinder

100 g/½ cup ground almonds

4 egg whites

pinch of salt

OPTION TWO: FRUIT FILLING

1 kg/2¼ lbs fruit of your choice

1–2 tablespoons sugar

STREUSEL TOPPING

300 g/2⅓ cups plain/all-purpose white wheat flour

200 g/13 tablespoons slightly chilled butter, cubed

100 g/½ cup sugar

TO FINISH

100 g/6½ tablespoons butter, melted

pinch of ground cinnamon

25 g/2 tablespoons sugar

square or round baking pan, about 30 cm/12 inches across, greased and floured

MAKES 1 BIG CAKE

Making a predough
Put 100 g/½ cup of the flour into a big bowl and make a well. Add the yeast and sugar to the well and pour in the milk. Cover and allow to rest for 1 hour.

Making the dough
Beat the predough together well with a big spoon. Add the egg yolks, sugar, salt and butter to the bowl and beat well again.

Add the remaining flour gradually, stopping when you have a soft dough that you can handle – but only just. Cover with clingfilm/plastic wrap and allow to rest for 1 hour.

Option One: poppy-seed filling
Put the milk, sugar, lemon zest and custard powder in a saucepan and bring to the boil, stirring constantly so it does not over-boil or burn on the bottom of the pan. Lower the heat and add the poppy seeds. Simmer, stirring constantly, for 10 minutes.

Remove from the heat and add the ground almonds. Stir, cover and allow to cool completely – about 1 hour.

Option Two: fruit filling
Wash the fruit of your choice. If you are using stone fruit (plums, peaches, apricots, etc.) slice them in half and remove the stone. Cut them in half (for plums and apricots) or into thick slices (peaches) and set aside.

If you are using apples, peel and core them. Slice them into thick slices and put them in water in which you have squeezed ½ lemon so that they do not go brown. Set aside.

If you are using strawberries, hull and halve them. Set aside.

If you are using smaller fruit, eg. raspberries or red currants, leave them whole and set aside.

Making the streusel topping
Mix the flour and sugar in a big bowl. Add the cubes of butter and rub in with your fingertips until you get crumbs. Cover and set aside.

Assembly for Option One: poppy-seed filling

Preheat the oven to 180°C (350°F) Gas 4.

With wet hands (so you don't stick), pull the dough out of the bowl directly into the prepared baking pan and gently press it down into the base. It should only be about ½ cm/¼ inch thick. Cover with a tea towel and allow to rest for 15 minutes.

While the dough is resting, put the egg whites and salt in a bowl and whisk until they form stiff peaks. Fold them into the cooked poppy-seed mixture until incorporated.

Spread the poppy-seed filling evenly over the dough with a spoon or a spatula. [1]

Scatter the streusel topping over the filling. [2]

Bake in the preheated oven for 35 minutes until the topping is golden brown.

To finish, while the cake is still hot, drizzle the melted butter over the top. Mix together the cinnamon and sugar and sprinkle these over the butter. Allow to cool completely before cutting.

Assembly for Option Two: fruit filling

Preheat the oven to 180°C (350°F) Gas 4.

With wet hands (so you don't stick), gently pull the dough out of the bowl directly into the prepared baking pan and gently press it down into the base. It should only be about ½ cm/ ¼ inch thick.

Press the prepared fruit firmly into the dough and sprinkle some sugar over it to make the juices run. Cover with a tea towel and allow to rest for 30 minutes.

Scatter the streusel topping over the filling.

Bake in the preheated oven for 35 minutes until the topping is golden brown.

To finish, while the cake is still hot, drizzle the melted butter over the top. Mix together the cinnamon and sugar and sprinkle these over the butter. Allow to cool completely before cutting.

index

author's acknowledgments

Thanks to:
Lucy for convincing me that bread is cool.
Erlend for always being encouraging.
All the bakers around the world from whom I continue to learn every day.

picture credits